FLYING SCOTSMAN

SCOTSMAN

The World's Most Travelled Steam Locomotive

PETER NICHOLSON

Ian Allan
PUBLISHING

First published 1999

ISBN 0 7110 2744 7

Published by Ian Allan Publishing

an imprint of Ian Allan Publishing Ltd,
Terminal House, Shepperton, Surrey TW17 8AS.
Printed by Ian Allan Printing Ltd,
Riverdene Business Park, Hersham, Surrey KT12 4RG

Code: 9911/B

Above: OO gauge model of No 60103 *Flying Scotsman* in
BR green livery, by Hornby, catalogue No R2020.
Courtesy Hornby Hobbies Ltd

This Page: A classic view of No 4472 *Flying Scotsman* as it
makes its historic departure from London, King's Cross
station on 1 May 1928 for the first nonstop run to
Edinburgh. It is interesting to note that no headboard
was carried on this occasion. *Ian Allan Library*

CONTENTS

Front cover: No 4472 is seen back on its old patch, the East Coast main line. *Flying Scotsman* emerges from Gaswork Tunnel, just to the north of Kings Cross station, on 4 July 1999 whilst hauling a special to York. *Brian Morrison*

Back cover: Flying Scotsman at Twickenham in July 1969 just before shipment to the USA. No buckeye or cowcatcher for this working but the bell and whistle can be seen.

ACKNOWLEDGEMENTS

As well as thanking those who have helped with the supply of information and photographs I would like to acknowledge those who have made the *Flying Scotsman* story possible. First and foremost of course, is Alan Pegler, without whom the story would have stopped abruptly at the end of Chapter 1! Alan has a remarkable memory for the facts and details regarding 'his' locomotive — as I am sure it will always be regarded with affection. Thanks also to the Hon Sir William McAlpine Bt for his major part in the story, to Pete Waterman for suggesting this book be produced in the first place and for adding a touch of controversy to the proceedings at times, and to Dr A. F. Marchington for ensuring the story continues.

Photographers are individually credited in the captions but I would like to thank them all for taking the trouble to provide suitable illustrations from their collections and for letting me retain these photographs for the considerable duration of completing this book, and getting it into print; in some cases it has run to a number of years. Ron White of Colour-Rail calls for particular mention for his superb service, not only to authors and publishers, but for ensuring the preservation of colour images which might otherwise simply have faded away. Others deserving of recognition for their assistance are Val Buddin, formerly Secretary of the Flying Scotsman Association; David Clifford; Roland Kennington; the Llangollen Railway; Richard Lucraft and John Slater, Chris Milner and Nick Pigott of *The Railway Magazine*; Brian Topping and David Ward. Thanks are also due to Dilip Sarkar and M. J. F. Bowyer whose names could well be appearing in a railway book for the first time as both are well-known *aviation* experts and who have provided detailed information on the presentation Spitfire aircraft, perhaps the least known snippets of information within these pages.

Thanks are extended to Darryl Reach of Haynes Publishing for encouragement in getting the initial book proposal underway and now to my new publishers for their support after acquiring the imprint that originally intended to publish the book. Therefore thanks to Nick Grant, Editor, and Peter Waller, Publishing Manager, for allowing unlimited access to the Ian Allan Library for photographs — previously considered to be 'out of bounds' and a great help in illustrating the manuscript. Particular acknowledgement is due to Alan Peglar again, for reading and approving the draft manuscript, and to Francis Blake for his careful reading of the manuscript at all stages from the first, very rough draft, and for comments and suggestions made. If anyone feels they should have been included in the above list please accept my apologies and assurance that this does not lessen the importance of their contributions to this story. The collection of information and illustrations will continue and it is hoped it will be possible to publish a new edition in the not-too-distant future to include the locomotive's travels in the early years of the 21st century.

Other books by the same author

The Barry Album
The Barry Locomotive Phenomenon (with Francis Blake)
Billy's Way Up (with W. J. Thomas)
The Fred Dibnah Album
Fred Dibnah Steams On (with Fred Dibnah)
Diesel Locomotives in Preservation Vols 1 and 2
From Font to Footplate (with Rev E. R. Boston)
The Honeybourne Line (with Colin Maggs)
Industrial Narrow Gauge Railways in Britain
Rising Steam

INTRODUCING THE LEGEND

'Alan! Come along Alan. There's a lot more to see.' The words drifted high up into the roof of the huge exhibition hall while the small boy stood there, mesmerised. Before him was the most wonderful thing he had ever seen. It towered above him, looking powerful, immaculate and exciting. He had seen many other railway engines, but only from station platforms, while this one, which was bigger than any he had seen before, was being viewed from ground level. The wheels were huge with highly polished rims and the bright green boiler was so long he could not even see the other end from where he was standing. As he looked up he was just about able to read the name in brass letters on a large curved plate over the centre driving wheels — *Flying Scotsman*.

This was an encounter the boy, who will feature again in this story when he is older, was never to forget and from that moment on he would often think about the impressive sight this locomotive had made when he had visited the British Empire Exhibition at Wembley in 1924. The exhibition was a major landmark in British history and was to prove extremely popular with the general public. Staged in London just six years after the end of World War 1, it was visited by many thousands of people from around the world and so successful was it in fact, that after the planned opening period from April to November 1924, a second, similar exhibition was held at the same venue the following year. The then recently formed and publicity conscious London & North Eastern Railway (LNER) had not only laid a loop line and opened a station to serve the exhibition but had also seized the opportunity for some major promotion of their Anglo-Scottish express train services. For this they had been only too pleased to provide one of their latest steam locomotives for static display, this carrying the name of their most famous 'crack' express, the 'Flying Scotsman'. This train was currently being advertised heavily in competition with the rival West Coast route services of the London, Midland & Scottish Railway (LMS).

The use of the same name for a locomotive as the passenger train has caused much confusion over the years through to the present day, some it has to be said, not entirely without commercial mischievousness on occasions. The 10am departure from London King's Cross to Edinburgh Waverley was a train that most people knew due to the LNER's

No 4472, as specially prepared for exhibition at Wembley in 1924. *Gresley Society Collection*

efficient publicity, so when told by the new owner of the locomotive, when he acquired it for preservation in the 1960s, that it was 'the world's most famous locomotive' this claim was perfectly acceptable. They had indeed heard the name before and, apart from Stephenson's *Rocket* perhaps, there were few other, if any, contenders for such a title. Since then it is the much-travelled locomotive that has become world famous, so when the new Great North Eastern Railway (GNER) was launched in 1996 under rail privatisation to operate the East Coast main line, and their rolling stock given the inscription 'The Route of the Flying Scotsman' it was perhaps the worldwide fame of the locomotive that was now being used, in part! That misunderstandings occur is obvious when the locomotive comes up in conversation and someone chips in, 'Oh, yes, I remember that locomotive — I went up to Scotland on it as a child...'

The origin of the name 'Flying Scotsman' has never really been explained however, and it was not used officially for the famous 10 o'clock train until the railway Grouping of 1923. Prior to that it was simply the term used by the staff to refer to their long-established prestige working. The locomotive, as we have seen, was named to publicise the train, but where did that get its name from? The 10am King's Cross departure dates right back to June 1862 and was initially referred to as the 'Special Scotch Express'. Later, it became known as the 'Flying Scotchman', the latter word being claimed by some to be a more

technically correct expression to use when referring to a person from Scotland than Scotsman. However, it is now no longer used due, no doubt, to its connotation with a certain malted drink. One theory is that the name, Flying Scotchman, or Scotsman, is simply a derivation from the earlier 'Flying Dutchman'. That was the name of a ship that set sail from Amsterdam back in 1680 but was lost at sea. The legend says that because the captain had defied God by continuing his voyage around the Cape of Good Hope despite a severe gale warning, he was condemned to roam the seas for ever. If that is the case, then, as *Flying Scotsman* is also destined to travel on for ever, it is a most appropriate name.

This is not a technical account of the locomotive and, in fact, it will not even mention such intimate details as the fact that it had a 'soot blower' fitted during its general repair in 1929. What will be recalled are its records and unique achievements, any significant changes in outward appearance, its worldwide travels, the key people who have been involved with the locomotive over the years and how it has been featured by the media as its fame has grown. In other words, the what and why of *Flying Scotsman's* claim to fame. Inevitably there will be much information familiar to railway enthusiasts — it could not be otherwise if the story is to be complete — but even they should find a few twists and turns in the story that they may not have heard or realised before. Therefore, this is the story, so far, of a locomotive that has had an immensely more interesting and exciting career than any other in the world, and is one with many more chapters still to come!

SOUVENIR

British Railways Board
Western Region
CARDIFF (Gen)
PLATFORM TICKET 1/-
Visit of
locomotive No. 4472.
'Flying Scotsman'
on March 18th 1964.

4472

SOUVENIR

Above:
The most famous locomotive nameplate in the world. The plaque beneath commemorates the world nonstop distance record for steam achieved by the locomotive on 8 August 1989 when it ran 422 miles 7.59 chains from Parkes to Broken Hill in Australia with a journey time of 9hr 25min. *Author*

Left:
Owners past and present: Alan Pegler, left, who saved the locomotive from certain destruction in 1963, and Dr Tony Marchington who has brought the locomotive back to life for the new millennium. They were photographed together at the National Railway Museum, York, June 1997. *Author*

Flying Scotsman is 'the most famous locomotive in the world', but is this claim *really* deserved or justified? Well, it does have some remarkable records and achievements to its name, but many of these have come about in recent years *because* the locomotive was already declared to be 'famous'. It is certainly the most travelled locomotive of all time. As an aside, although in some quarters it is traditional to refer to steam locomotives in the feminine gender, it does not always seem quite right for an engine with such a masculine name, so, in most cases 'it' will be used, although as one owner always referred to No 4472 as the 'old girl', the occasional 'she' or 'her' may creep into the narrative.

Not long after having been absorbed into British Railways' stock at Nationalisation in 1948, *Flying Scotsman* was given the anonymous number 60103 and as such was considered as being no more than just another main line engine and one of 78 virtually identical members of the 'A3' class. It retained this numeric identity, along with its *Flying Scotsman* nameplates, until withdrawn in January 1963, when precisely 40 years old. It could then have so easily met the same fate as the rest of the class and most other steam locomotives, its various achievements becoming no more than footnotes in detailed locomotive history books. By today it would be all but forgotten except by knowledgeable students of railway history. Many other locomotives with claims to fame, including speed records and other 'firsts', have gone this way. In the late 1980s, Philip Atkins of the National Railway Museum undertook research to establish the total number of steam locomotives built, worldwide. The result came out at about 660,000.

THE GRESLEY PACIFICS

No 4472, sometimes No 60103, is often referred to as a Gresley Pacific and, unless you know, this might not mean a lot, but to others such a description is almost magical. Herbert Nigel Gresley was the head of the design team that produced this and many other successful and attractive-looking locomotives. The wheel arrangement of this particular class was 4-6-2, and went by the name of Pacific. This comprised six large driving wheels with four smaller weight-bearing wheels at the front and two more at the back, under the cab. The tender, for coal and water, was coupled up behind the engine, the

Flying Scotsman was neither unique nor the first of its type. The first Gresley-designed 'A1' class Pacific was No 4470 *Great Northern*, seen here with a much earlier predecessor from East Coast main line express passenger services, Stirling Single No 1 of 1870.
Real Photographs/Ian Allan Library

wheels of this not being included in the designation. At first, *Flying Scotsman* was given the LNER classification of 'A1', but for a while was redesignated 'A10' until becoming Class A3 after certain modifications were made.

Although it was the third example of the 'A1' class to be built, *Flying Scotsman* came into the world claiming a 'first'. During the time of its construction at Doncaster Works the London & North Eastern Railway had come into being on 1 January 1923 through the amalgamation of a number of railway companies and was part of the Grouping, the result of the Railways Act of 1921 which merged 120 separate undertakings into just four railways. This happened to be the first locomotive to be completed and enter traffic under the auspices of the LNER, although construction had been started late the previous year when Doncaster was still the works of the Great Northern Railway (GNR).

SIR NIGEL GRESLEY

Gresley was appointed Locomotive Superintendent of the Great Northern Railway in 1911, having previously been the Superintendent of the Carriage & Wagon Department. He was an innovative engineer and it was not long after World War 1 that he started developing locomotives for a new age, larger and more powerful than any ever seen before on a British railway. The GNR used a logical method of classification for its locomotives, with each wheel arrangement given a different letter followed by a number to distinguish the various types with the same layout. Thus a six-coupled, or 0-6-0, engine was a 'J', Gresley designing the Class J38 for example, while 'A' was retained for the 4-6-2 wheel arrangement as these were to be the prestige express passenger engines.

Few formal portraits of Sir Nigel Gresley exist; this was taken in a studio c1936.
Geoffrey Hughes Collection

Until 1922 only one Pacific had been produced in Great Britain, *The Great Bear,* built by the Great Western Railway (GWR) in 1908. That, it has to be said, was not a great success. It was subsequently rebuilt as a 4-6-0 and was a type never to be produced again by the GWR, although the other three railways of the 'Big Four' — the LNER, LMS and Southern — were all to adopt this arrangement for locomotives to be used on express train services.

A locomotive engineer is never free to design motive power to satisfy his own desires. (Although a pupil of Sir Nigel didn't do too badly in this respect on another railway later, but that is another story...) The locomotive has to be produced to carry out a particular job of work, that is pulling trains of a certain weight, for specified distances at the required speed. Having established this requirement, the machine then has to fit within the loading gauge which is determined by the height of bridges and tunnels and the width between station platforms on the line, while it must not exceed the weight per axle as specified by the civil engineers responsible for the track.

The East Coast main line (ECML) which links the capitals of England and Scotland has always been Britain's principal railway route and motive power for use on these services has seen a steady progression right from the earliest days of railways. The Great Northern 'Singles', the 4-2-2s designed by Patrick Stirling, were the racehorses of their day, and were replaced by Henry Ivatt's 4-4-2 Atlantics in 1902 and so by 1922, it was inevitable that their successors should be 4-6-2 Pacifics. Gresley's design was also a logical development from some of his earlier work. The days of the GNR as an independent railway were already numbered when the first of Gresley's Pacifics emerged from Doncaster Works —

the 'Plant' as it was always known to railwaymen — in April 1922. Numbered 1470 it carried the name *Great Northern* on large curved brass nameplates either side of the engine, a most unusual feature for this railway as it had only once before bestowed a name on a locomotive, in that case, Ivatt Atlantic No 990 *Henry Oakley* of 1898.

Later the same month, *Great Northern* was sent south to King's Cross for display and it was a sensation. Not only was it so much larger than its predecessors, it was also so beautifully proportioned with very graceful lines and finished in a stunning apple green livery, lined in black and white with dark green edging on the tender. Gresley had produced a visual masterpiece. So good were its lines that, even today, it must be regarded by most as being exactly what an express steam locomotive *should* look like. No 1470 was quickly followed by No 1471 *Sir Frederick Banbury*, completed in July 1922 and named at the end of the year after the GNR's last Chairman. Not long after these two locomotives had entered service Doncaster Works received an order for 10 more examples of the 'A1' class, to be numbered 1472-81.

The date 1 January 1923 is one of the most significant in British railway history as it was then that the majority of Britain's railways were grouped into the four privately owned companies — the 'Big Four' as they were known. The Great Western Railway in effect merely absorbed a number of smaller railways but the Southern, the London, Midland & Scottish and London & North Eastern railways were entirely new concerns, each made up of railways of varying sizes and importance, largely in separate geographical areas. The principal companies making up the LNER were, in addition to the Great Northern: the North Eastern, Great Eastern, Great Central and Hull & Barnsley in England and the North British and Great North of Scotland, north of the Border. Each of these railways had their own Locomotive Superintendent, or Chief Mechanical Engineer, but of course there was only one such vacancy in the new company. This prestigious position was offered to John Robinson from the Great Central, but at 66 years of age he recommended that Gresley, 20 years his junior, be given the job. Few would dispute the wisdom of this suggestion.

No 1472 — THE FIRST PRODUCTION 'A1'

The main frames for the first of the 10 production 'A1' class Pacifics ordered by the GNR were produced in October 1922. This was to be No 1472, although at this stage no name had been allocated. When the steel for the two main frame members was first rolled, their sheer size meant that inevitably they were not perfectly flat. In order to straighten them to the perfection and accuracy required for

assembly they were beaten by hand with the peen of a hammer in carefully chosen areas by highly skilled men to de-stress the metal and to ensure that the plates were completely flat. The marks so made, looking not unlike a snail had slithered all over the metal, became visible again during the locomotive's recent very thorough overhaul at Southall and were pointed out to visitors

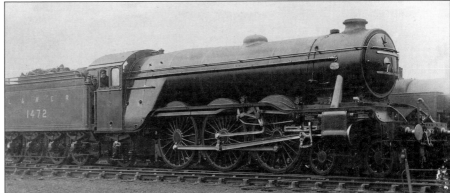

The newly completed No 1472, as built in 1923 and yet to be named, renumbered or given the brass edges to its splashers. *Ian Allan Library*

by Roland Kennington who is today responsible for the maintenance of this thoroughbred.

No 1472 was not completed until the new year, by which time the GNR had been absorbed into the new concern so that when it was rolled out this locomotive displayed brass plates affixed to either side of the smokebox proudly proclaiming its parentage as the new LNER. The works No 1564 was also carried although this was in fact the 1,553rd locomotive built at Doncaster since works No 1 in 1867 as the 10 numbers, 1554-63, had not been used. Ultimately, Doncaster was to complete a total of 2,223 steam locomotives, including 212 of various standard designs for BR after Nationalisation in 1948, the very last appearing from the 'Plant' in 1957.

It was on 7 February that No 1472 formally saw the light of day and, like its two predecessors, looked simply superb. The lined apple green livery was similar to that used by *Great Northern* but the tender was now lettered 'L&NER' with the number 1472 beneath. The cost of the locomotive and tender was recorded as being £7,944. The railway wasted no time in seeking further publicity and No 1472 was despatched to London for display at Marylebone station on 22 February. Just two days later it officially entered service and was allocated to Doncaster motive power depot. Later in the year it was joined at Doncaster by four more 'A1s', with another two being based at King's Cross shed and a further three at Grantham. With their reliability and much increased power over their predecessors, these 10 engines really did improve the service on the southern end of the East Coast main line.

No 1472 ON TRIAL

Still unnamed, No 1472 was picked from the 12 'A1s' so far built to undertake comparative trials in June and July 1923. It was pitched against another Pacific type that had been developed just prior to the Grouping by the North Eastern Railway (NER) to the design of Sir Vincent Raven. Two of these less graceful looking locomotives had been completed by the time the LNER came into being and it was considered only fair that the two classes of 4-6-2 inherited by the railway should be compared for power and efficiency before further construction took place. Former NER No 2400 *City of Newcastle* and No 1472 were selected to work the two hardest duties on the ECML in turn. These were the 10.51am Doncaster to King's Cross and the 5.40pm return, made up of portions for several destinations in Yorkshire and Lincolnshire, as well as the dynamometer car in each case to record the locomotive's performance. The trials were conducted between 25 June and 4 July, with test runs being made on nine days. Extensive information and data was gleaned from these trials and analysed, particularly with regard to coal and water consumption. The results were reported to Gresley on 21 July by means of a memo, and suffice to say, he took this as the go-ahead to continue with his own Pacifics, and a further 40 were then ordered. No 1472 had proved its superiority over the Raven Pacific, just, although there were indications in the information gleaned that perhaps there was room for improvement.

A NEW IDENTITY AND FAME AWAITS

On 27 December 1923 No 1472 returned to the place of its birth for a general repair. It appears that while in service its centre piston rod had been fractured and a replacement was required before it could return to traffic. However, there was not a spare available and so it was for this reason that this particular locomotive was selected for an unusual duty — to represent the LNER as a static exhibit in the Palace of Engineering at the forthcoming British Empire Exhibition, to be held at Wembley. As such it would be away from the action on the main line for the best part of the year.

The LNER decided to take full advantage of the publicity opportunity and spent the next couple of months preparing the locomotive for its prestigious but non-active appearance. During this time, in February 1924, a new numbering scheme was introduced which involved the numbers of all former Great Northern engines being increased by 3,000 so that this example became No 4472. Although not then considered in any way distinctive, this number has since become possibly the most famous engine number of all time. However, the name chosen, specifically for this display locomotive, was even then considered to be the most famous *train* in the world — *Flying Scotsman*.

A number of non-standard embellishments were added to No 4472 during this cosmetic overhaul, including the fitting of brass beading to the splashers and boiler washout plugs, while the wheel rims and axle ends were highly polished and the new company coat of arms was applied to the cab side. The effect was stunning. It certainly impressed that small boy mentioned earlier, as it did all who saw her there. It was the largest locomotive on display and its brightly polished apple green livery, scarlet buffer beams and brasswork left one in no doubt that this was the star attraction among the engineering exhibits.

Not far from *Flying Scotsman* in the exhibition hall was another engine, impressive but nothing like as imposing as the Gresley Pacific and noticeably smaller. This was the Great Western Railway's 4-6-0 No 4073 *Caerphilly Castle*. However, it carried a notice which did attract attention. It simply read, 'Britain's most powerful passenger locomotive'. That was not what the LNER publicity department had wanted to see, and they were not best pleased!

The British Empire Exhibition was officially opened by HM King George V in May 1924 and No 4472 was in residence at Wembley from then until 1 November. During this time the LNER produced a souvenir booklet on the locomotive which included a set of working drawings and a detailed specification. This was to be the first of several books specifically on this locomotive which is, in itself, an interesting facet of its claim to fame. A colour print of the locomotive was also produced for the exhibition and, again, was the first of many that have appeared depicting this particular locomotive over the years.

EXHIBITION REPERCUSSIONS

The statement that Charles Collett's smaller 'Castle' class 4-6-0 (a popular and common wheel arrangement that perhaps surprisingly was not given a name) was more powerful than the

Top:
Now carrying its new identity, which would become probably the most famous locomotive number in the world — No 4472 — and named *Flying Scotsman*, the 'A1' class Pacific is seen ready for placing on display at the British Empire Exhibition, Wembley, in 1924. Note the LNER crest is on the cab side and the number is on the tender. *W. J. Reynolds/ Ian Allan Library*

Above:
No 4472 in exhibition finish is seen at work on the East Coast main line in 1924. *Ian Allan Library*

11

LNER's 'A1' Pacifics could not be allowed to pass without challenge. Therefore, in April 1925 comparative trials were set up between the two railways. Nos 4074 *Caldicot Castle* and 4079 *Pendennis Castle* were readied by the GWR as were 'A1s' Nos 4474 (later named *Victor Wild*) and 4475 *Flying Fox* by the LNER. No 4079 came to King's Cross depot for the trials, while No 4474 went over to Old Oak Common on the GWR. The trials were conducted between 27 April and 2 May. The results were startling. On the Great Western's line from Paddington to Plymouth, the LNER locomotive performed well, particularly on the notorious South Devon banks, and kept to time. But coal consumption was no less than 14% greater than the GWR's own engine on the same journey, and the 'Castle' managed to arrive a quarter of an hour early!

On the LNER's home ground, the GWR engine still managed to reduce coal consumption noticeably and ran to better time than the native engine. The outcome of these trials was that Gresley made modifications to the valve gear and later, fitted higher pressure boilers which resulted in the reclassification of the 'A1s' to Class A3, the type by which *Flying Scotsman* is known today. Although the latter has so often been the locomotive chosen for prestigious events and occasions it is probably just as well, from a publicity point of view, that No 4472 was not available for the slightly embarrassing trials of 1925.

RETURN TO WEMBLEY

The success of the British Empire Exhibition in 1924 resulted in it being re-staged in 1925. The opportunity was taken to commemorate the 100th anniversary of the opening of the Stockton & Darlington Railway, the first locomotive-worked public railway in the world and an ancestor of the LNER. This section of the exhibition was entitled 'Centenary of British Railways' and No 4472 was again chosen for display. In between its two exhibition appearances it had undergone a heavy repair at Doncaster arriving at Wembley in March. This time it was coupled to a shorter, six-wheeled tender borrowed from one of Gresley's 'K3' class 2-6-0s because of limited display space in the exhibition hall. This tender was, of course, painted and lettered to match the locomotive with the number 4472 on its sides.

Flying Scotsman remained on show at Wembley until the end of October and, because of this, it was not available for participation in the Railway Centenary cavalcade that took place in July in County Durham. The GWR chose to exhibit No 4079 *Pendennis Castle* at Wembley as they, too, never liked to miss an opportunity for publicity. Subsequently these two locomotives have met up on several notable occasions, including a historic meeting at a most unlikely venue on the other side of the world, as described later.

When No 4472 re-entered traffic after the second Wembley exhibition it retained some of its embellishments, the cab-side coat of arms lasting until 1928, and it was not until 1938 that the brass

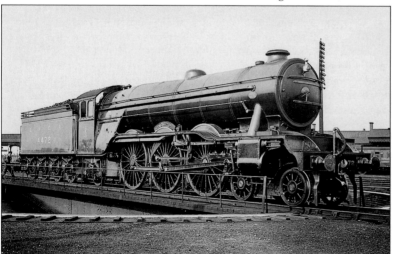

splasher trims were painted over. At one time Gresley is said to have made a suggestion that a few selected celebrity locomotives should be given red-backed nameplates rather than black but this idea was never implemented. *Flying Scotsman* was naturally a contender for this treatment but had to wait some considerable time before this distinctive feature was adopted.

Depicted at Grantham in 1927, the locomotive still sported its exhibition features.
T. G. Hepburn/Ian Allan Library

LONDON TO EDINBURGH NONSTOP

While the GWR and LNER had been rivals in the exhibition hall, it was on the track that the LMS and LNER showed their competitiveness. There had been a long-running battle between the West and East Coast routes linking London and Scotland, but since the end of the previous century the respective railway companies had honoured an agreement not to compete with each other regarding journey times because of safety considerations. Trains had become increasingly more comfortable and the distance they could run nonstop was constantly under review, although even this did not allow them to reduce overall journey times. The LMS had managed to achieve regular nonstop running between London

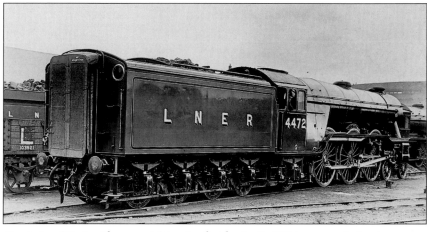

No 4472 is seen newly fitted with a corridor tender in April 1928.
Gresley Society Collection

Euston and Carlisle Kingmoor with its 'Royal Scot' class 4-6-0s — a distance of 301.1 miles. The LNER therefore aimed to beat this once and for all by running from London King's Cross, all the way to Edinburgh Waverley — no less than 392.7 miles without stopping. This would be a world record, and with a journey time of 8hr, would be more than one crew of driver and fireman could perform. Gresley had come up with the idea of the locomotive being fitted with a special tender that had a corridor passing through it, alongside the water tank and connecting with the first coach of the train so that the crew could be changed en route.

The story has been told that Gresley, who was quite a large man, tried out his theory for the corridor tender in his dining room at home. He arranged the dining chairs in a row along the wall with a small gap in between. When his daughter Violet suddenly entered the room she was somewhat startled to see her father squeezing his way behind the chairs and thought he must have entered a second childhood! From this experiment he considered that the corridor would need to be no more than 18in wide by 5ft high.

Two locomotives were equipped with the new corridor tenders in April 1928. One of these was No 4472, the other being No 4476 *Royal Lancer*. *Flying Scotsman* was fresh from a general repair at Doncaster which had included the fitting of longer travel valve gear as a result of the findings from the trials with the GWR 'Castles'. This improvement achieved a considerable saving of coal. A Gresley Pacific hauling a 500-ton train for example, would now consume only 38lb per mile compared with 50lb previously, thus making the nonstop London to Edinburgh train feasible. These two 'A1s' also had a reduction made to their overall height by fitting slightly shorter chimneys, steam dome covers, safety valves and whistles with the cab roofs lowered similarly and the cab footsteps reduced in width. This was necessary because, being one of the original members of the class, No 4472 had been built, it will be remembered, to the maximum loading gauge of the old Great Northern Railway and *not* to work all the way through to Scotland. Now this, and other members of the class, would be working all the way up the East Coast main line, nonstop to Edinburgh, so their journey would take in the sections originally operated by the old North Eastern and North British railways which had not shared the GNR's particularly generous loading gauge. It was on emerging from this overhaul at Doncaster that No 4472 lost its cab-side company crest. Before returning to traffic it travelled 'up' to London once again for showing off to the press. It was already becoming a much-photographed locomotive.

The nonstop trains were scheduled to commence on 1 May 1928, and for these the LNER had produced entirely new passenger coaches which incorporated a number of additional amenities, particularly with the ladies in mind, such as a hairdressing compartment. The services to have the benefit of this new stock were the simultaneous 'Flying Scotsman' 10am departures from King's Cross and Waverley. It was of course most fitting that for the inaugural run the locomotive and train should carry the same name. The southbound train, which was worked on the first day by sister engine No 2580 *Shotover*, was completely overshadowed by the northbound working as most media coverage, as ever, was concentrated at London. The inaugural 'down' train, which weighed a total of 386 tons, had Driver Pibworth of King's Cross shed at the controls from London where there was a civic send off attended by the Lord Mayor of London. The interest from the public was considerable and there were so many spectators at King's Cross that morning that the railway officials had difficulty in getting through to the engine!

As the train reached Alne in Northumberland, almost exactly 200 miles from London, the crew was suddenly joined on the footplate by Driver Blades of Gateshead with his fireman, to take over duties for the second half of the journey to Edinburgh. After an exchange of pleasantries and an update on the locomotive's performance, the London crew made their way through the tender for a well-earned rest 'on the cushions' in the front coach of the train where a compartment was reserved for the loco crews. The total journey time was 8hr 3min. No 4472 worked back down to London the next day on the 'up' (in railway jargon) 'Flying Scotsman', but with rather less public and media attention.

The whole exercise had been a huge promotional success with stations all along the route lined with people waving to the train as it passed by. This first run of a world record-breaking service has subsequently contributed much to the fame of No 4472 and the event has since been commemorated on notable anniversaries. The service was of great interest to the public of the day, although it was 'record breaking' only because it was to be a regular service. The LMS had in a way stolen the

A magnificent view of No 4472 *Flying Scotsman* setting off from King's Cross on 1 May 1928 with the first nonstop train to Edinburgh. The surrounding publicity set the locomotive on the course of fame, which has grown ever since. *Ian Allan Library*

LNER's thunder as they had run the 'Royal Scot' train nonstop from London Euston to Edinburgh and Glasgow (399.7 and 401.4 miles respectively) on 27 April. The train had been run in two portions, one to each destination, but this was just a one-off demonstration. Ironically, as the agreement over competing with time was still in existence from the end of the previous century, any nonstop services still had to slow down at some point to spin out the actual travelling time so as not to arrive too early! Therefore, the LNER's 'customers', or passengers as they were then more accurately described, would not have suffered any delay if the train *had* stopped very briefly en route for a quick crew change. This would have avoided the considerable costs involved in the construction of the special tenders and of crews travelling twice the distance of their working route and being paid to be passengers. But the public loved the idea of the 'nonstop' journey and for this reason it was considered a valuable publicity exercise and therefore well worth while. (A similar example today perhaps, albeit on a somewhat larger scale, is the construction of a dedicated railway line between the Channel Tunnel and north London. In reality, this will almost certainly not actually speed up total journey times very much, particularly for those starting from, or whose destinations are south of the River Thames, but it would no doubt help to sell seats on the trains nevertheless and show that anything the French can do, so can the British...)

FLYING SCOTSMAN, FILM STAR

No 4472 has the great distinction of starring in what has been claimed to be the first British-made feature film with sound. Entitled *The Flying Scotsman* this was made in 1929 and released in 1930 by British International Pictures. Directed by Castleton Knight it was originally going to be a silent film but the technology for 'talkies' was being developed at that time so the last two reels were made as sound-on-film and it was promoted as 'part talking'. (The earlier Al Jolson films, such as *The Jazz Singer*, had used a cumbersome sound-on-disc system which soon became obsolete.)

Carrying the 'Flying Scotsman' headboard, No 4472 awaits a filming session as 'K2' class 2-6-0 No 4668 is fitted with a camera for line-to-line shooting. *Ian Allan Library*

In the film the loco driver is shown as a drunk who nearly wrecks the Scottish express and in one scene the engine is seen breaking away from the train, and continuing on its journey alone. The locomotive used throughout was appropriately, No 4472, with many scenes shot between King's Cross and Edinburgh, so the LNER connection was obvious to all, but this was not quite the publicity the company wanted. Gresley was not amused. In fact, he insisted that a disclaimer be included in the film titles stating: 'Dramatic licence has been taken for film purposes and does not represent the actual safety equipment used by the LNER.' The film starred Pauline Johnson with Ray Milland as the fireman and Moore Marriott as the driver who is probably best known today for his part in the classic 1937 film, *Oh! Mr Porter*. The filming of No 4472 took place on Sunday mornings on the Hertford Loop line, with additional scenes shot between Crews Hill, Cuffley and Bayford, and by Stapleford signalbox.

GOING FOR THE TON

In 1933, Germany had introduced the 'Flying Hamburger', a diesel-electric train which connected Berlin with Hamburg, covering the 178 miles in 2hr 18min at an average speed of 77.4mph. Gresley went to Germany the following year, travelled on this service and discussed the possibilty of the Germans producing a similar three-car train for the King's Cross-Newcastle service. The German engineers made a study of the East Coast main line and reported that such a train would require 4$\frac{1}{2}$hr for the 268 miles and would accommodate 140 passengers, but not in the same comfort as existing trains and no hot meals could be served. Gresley, and the LNER management, were not impressed.

Gresley was therefore granted the go-ahead to see just what one of his Pacifics could do if given the chance. Almost inevitably, the locomotive chosen for this trial run was No 4472 *Flying Scotsman* and this was to go down in history as one of its greatest ever claims to fame. The well-known railway historian, the late O. S. Nock, stated that *Flying Scotsman* was never one of the best of the London-based Pacifics and the running staff at King's Cross would have preferred to have used either No 4474 *Victor Wild* or No 4475 *Flying Fox*. But this was intended to be a test to see what an 'average' locomotive could do and not an all-out world speed record attempt. This would come later. The test was set for 30 November 1934, the 147-ton train comprising four coaches (not the three of the German diesel). These were two standard passenger carriages, a restaurant car and the company's dynamometer car.

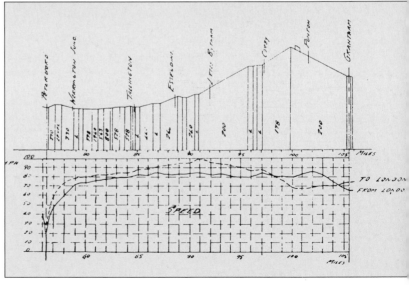

16

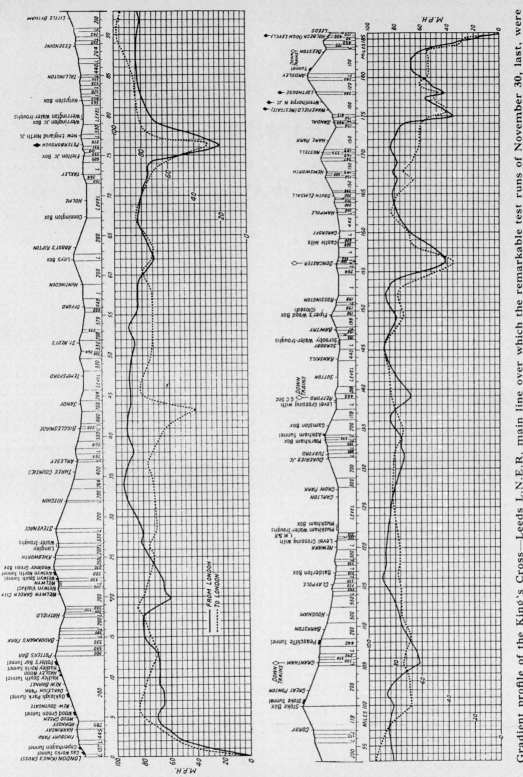

Gradient profile of the King's Cross—Leeds L.N.E.R. main line over which the remarkable test runs of November 30, last, were made at the speeds shown by the two graphs

Severe speed restrictions shown by black diamonds, slight restrictions by white diamonds

Opposite and above:
Graphs illustrating the gradients and speeds recorded on 30 November 1934. The magic '100' occurred midway between Little Bytham and Essendine, the dynamometer car recording this speed for a distance of 600 yards. *Courtesy The Railway Magazine*

On the footplate were Driver W. Sparshatt, Fireman R. Webster and Gresley's assistant, O. V. S. Bulleid, who later achieved immortality through his unique design of Pacific locomotive for the Southern Railway. On the train was Cecil J. Allen, the railway author and historian who was highly regarded for the accuracy of his train time recordings and probably travelled more miles by rail than any other enthusiast. Bill Sparshatt was *Flying Scotsman's* regular driver at this time and had already made a name for himself as being bit of a showman on the footplate and therefore an appropriate choice for this occasion.

The 'down' run to Leeds took 151min 56sec for the 185.8 miles, the highest speed recorded being 95mph. The journey time was to stand as the record for more than 30 years, and a best ever for steam traction. The return to London was made by the same crew, again with No 4472 and after only 2hr of rest time at Leeds. The train now had an additional two coaches and a maximum speed of precisely 100mph, the magic 'ton', was recorded on the chart in the dyamometer car as the train neared Little Bytham, Lincolnshire. This was officially claimed by the LNER as the first ever authenticated 100mph achieved by a steam locomotive and is a claim to fame that has meant much in the locomotive's history. The journey from Leeds to King's Cross had been completed in 157min 17sec giving an average speed, start to stop for the round trip of 72.2mph. This was a great coup for the LNER and a remarkable achievement by both locomotive and crew — particularly the fireman. No less than nine tons of coal were consumed on the return trip which works out at more than 4,000lb per hour — more than a third greater than what was later to be considered possible for a single fireman on a long run! This personal achievement, and the fact that No 4472 had burnt so much coal, was not so highly publicised by the LNER.

The figures recorded by the stop-watch of Cecil J. Allen do not in fact back up the 100mph claim. His timings were made from the carriage window and produced *average* quarter of a mile speeds but his calculations have been used on many occasions to substantiate journey timings and speeds. When his recordings from this run are examined the highest noted speed was just less than the ton — 98mph — but a study of the dynamometer car graph, as reproduced in *The Railway Magazine*, shows the top edge of the line indicating the speed as being *just* on the 100mph mark. Perhaps it is as well that a finer nib was not used... However, whatever the actual figure obtained, it was a spectacular run and one that will always stand as the first *official* three-figure speed achieved by a steam locomotive, claiming a well deserved place in railway history.

No 4472 was building up its reputation and the news of its 100mph achievement was broadcast to the nation by BBC radio on its 9 o'clock news that evening. The locomotive was also getting about the country too, or so it appeared, as it was depicted as the centrepiece of a number of seaside postcards showing a selection of local views and announcing the sender had 'Just arrived at...' These included such unlikely destinations for a LNER locomotive at that time, as Folkestone, Llandudno and Paignton, but many years later, some of these far flung places would indeed be reached by this very engine.

A 100mph FOOTNOTE

There had been for some time, another claimant to the first steam locomotive to reach 100mph. This was GWR 'City' class 4-4-0 No 3440 *City of Truro*, the date of this run being 9 March 1904 and the speed claimed on this dash from Plymouth to Paddington was no less than 102.3mph. This was logged by the famed 'railwayac' of the day, Charles Rous-Marten, who was a passenger on the train and made his calculations by observation from the carriage window, with stop-watch in hand. Therefore, we are here talking about an average time over a short distance rather than a very brief maximum peak, as with No 4472 more than 30 years later. This claim has for long been the subject of controversy and much debate amongst railway enthusiasts and historians. The accepted conclusions, after close study, is that the locomotive could well have achieved 100mph, and must have been pretty close even if it did not, but the fact is that the recorded figure is unproven. Therefore, if an accurate speed is not known for that occasion a record cannot be claimed officially. Although Rous-Marten was a much-respected train time recorder, however accurate he was with his stop-watch checking the travelling time at quarter-mile intervals, he could not possibly refine this method to 10ths of a mile per hour. He could perhaps have claimed 102, 102½ or even 103mph, but *not* 102.3.

It is surely remarkable in any case, that no less than three decades were to pass before any other steam locomotive in Britain came anywhere near to matching this speed. There was considerable development of steam traction taking place during these years and it seems incredible that on no other occasion between 1904 and 1934 did the opportunity arise or the conditions provide for a locomotive to attempt 100mph. It should be added that locomotives did not then have speedometers (or tachographs!) so if any service trains did get near the 'ton' there was no need for the driver to admit to what would probably have been an exceeding of a speed restriction. It is believed that drivers were sufficiently familiar with their routes and their locomotives to be able to assess their speed at any time very accurately, hence there was little priority given to installing any form of speed recording apparatus. Like *Flying Scotsman's* record it was nevertheless a remarkable achievement and the locomotive fully deserves its place in railway history. *City of Truro*, which incidentally just happened to be Swindon Works No 2000, is an example of a locomotive that has been preserved and has obtained legendary status because of its one high-speed run.

LESS OF THE LIMELIGHT

Following the epic and record breaking runs of November 1934, *Flying Scotsman* returned to routine duties from King's Cross and could well have seen out the rest of its days as just another of the 79 similar 'A1/A3' class Gresley Pacifics until meeting the same ultimate fate as the others. Although it had a few remarkable runs to its credit, by the time of its headline-hitting high-speed test run it had already clocked up well over half a million miles, most of which were on normal service trains.

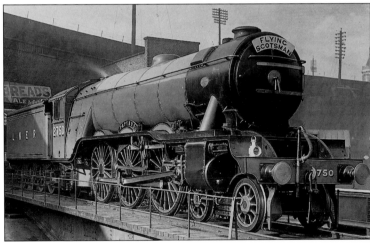

The last of the type to be built was No 2508 *Brown Jack*, emerging from Doncaster Works in January 1935 and there were many years of outstanding but day-to-day work ahead of the class. The next test run involving the class took place on 5 March 1935, this being a high-speed working from Newcastle upon Tyne to King's Cross, but the chosen locomotive was No 2750 *Papyrus*. On this occasion the highest speed reached and confirmed by the recording instruments was no less than 108mph, setting a new world speed record for steam traction. This was to prove the viability of high-speed, nonstop passenger services, as well as the fact that Gresley had been able to adopt the improvements resulting from the earlier comparative trials with the GWR engines. Unfortunately, poor old *Papyrus*, unlike other record breakers such as *Flying Scotsman* and *City of Truro*, was not saved from the knacker's yard when withdrawn from service and was unceremoniously broken up.

No 4472's recording breaking sister, No 2750 *Papyrus*, complete with 'Flying Scotsman' headboard. *Ian Allan Library*

All the original 'A1' class Pacifics were eventually brought up to 'A3' class standard but their prestigious days were soon to be eclipsed by Gresley's next express passenger class which incorporated all the lessons learned. These were the 'A4' streamlined Pacifics, of which the most famous was to be No 4468 *Mallard*, which to this day holds the world speed record for steam traction, at 126mph.

The 'A3s' continued to be used on the nonstop 'Flying Scotsman' train service throughout 1935, covering a total of 47,000 miles and on only two occasions did a late arrival occur. In both cases this was attributable to permanent way work. The following year saw the last working of the 'Flying Scotsman' train by an 'A3', the duty then being handed over to the new stars of the track, the 'A4s', or 'Streaks' as they have been known to generations of enthusiasts.

No 4472 was not to be forgotten entirely though, and made a number of appearances at local exhibitions staged by the LNER who realised she was still the railway's star locomotive, although the fact that its name was the same as the train they wished to promote obviously helped. Such appearances took the 'A1' Pacific to some out-of-the-way places for the type, including Stratford (London), Norwich and even Southend-on-Sea, but not, as yet, Llandudno or Paignton!

In March 1939 *Flying Scotsman* was transferred from King's Cross back to its original depot at Doncaster where it was to be based for most of the war period. On 5 April 1941, Gresley died suddenly following a heart attack, although he had not been in the best of health for some time and had never really got over the loss of his wife earlier. He had been knighted in 1936 and his name will live for ever through his contribution to railway engineering, with *Flying Scotsman* destined to be his best and most travelled ambassador.

Top:
No 4472 was always a popular locomotive at exhibitions and was displayed at an open day at Ilford Depot on 2 June 1934. On the left is 'P2' class 2-8-2 No 2001 *Cock o' the North*.
E. R. Wethersett/Ian Allan Library

Above:
No 4472, with non-corridor tender, at Doncaster on 2 July 1938, and Atlantics Nos 3280 and 3254 and 0-6-0 No 3073. *T. G. Hepburn/Rail Archive Stephenson*

In spring 1943 this celebrity locomotive emerged from Doncaster Works having received a general repair and now painted in an all-over wartime black livery, a far cry from its glory days. (This is one 'authentic' livery that is unlikely to be repeated in preservation; the response from many enthusiasts would be unprintable as they consider that even BR dark green is unbearable!) Like all main line locomotives at this time, express passenger engines were frequently to be found at the head of goods trains or troop specials, often working beyond their normal operating area.

In 1944 *Flying Scotsman* was moved around rather more than usual. In March it was transferred to New England depot at Peterborough, then to the former Great Central shed at Gorton, Manchester in July before returning in October to the more familiar territory of the ECML at King's Cross. However, two weeks later it was transferred again to New England then on to Doncaster in early December.

FLYING SCOTSMAN TAKES TO THE SKIES

During World War 2 many towns and organisations undertook fund raising to sponsor aircraft and armaments to help the war effort. Initially this was rather haphazard but after a while things became more organised and the official 'Spitfire Fund', for example, was set up and a number of towns, cities and groups in Britain and the Empire were able to have their name applied to a particular aircraft. Groups of employees from companies also participated in such fund raising and this included the LNER. The amount required to finance one Spitfire was £5,000 and the LNER was able to sponsor several aircraft. Known as presentation aircraft, they were not of course built specially but were selected from standard production runs and would therefore have been built anyway, but it helped people to know they were 'doing their bit' for the war effort.

The LNER financed two Spitfire Mk Is in 1940, one of which, serial number X4913, was given the name *Flying Scotsman*, a particularly suitable name for a plane. It can almost certainly be said to have been named after the locomotive, rather than the train, as the other, X4914, was inscribed *Cock o' the North*, after 'P2' class 2-8-2 No 2001. Unfortunately, X4913 was rather short-lived and came to a tragic end. Built by Vickers at Southampton its first flight took place on the last day of 1940 and it was delivered to No 411 Squadron at Digby, Lincolnshire three days later. There, it was replaced by a Spitfire IIa, and X4913 was then transferred on 22 June 1941 to 53 Operational Training Unit. Exactly one month later it failed to return from a training flight but it was not until November that year that the wreckage was found, this being in a remote spot high in the Brecon Beacons. The body of the pilot was recovered but it is said that some of the scattered aircraft parts can still be seen to this day.

In 1942 another Spitfire was to be honoured with the *Flying Scotsman* name and contributed much more to the Allied defences than its predecessor. Built by Vickers-Armstrong at Castle Bromwich, BM202 was a Spitfire Vb which was taken on charge by the RAF on 6 March, joining No 222 Squadron. From then until July it was active over France taking part in close escort and high cover to RAF Bostons on bombing raids. Various transfers took place during the summer, it joining No 242 Squadron and is recorded as having fought over Dieppe on 19 August but went for an overhaul in the autumn when the squadron was transferred to North Africa. Little is known of its later career and it was officially 'struck off charge' on 21 June 1947 but this was rather an arbitrary date as a vast number of unaccounted for aircraft were written off on that occasion. This particular plane was the subject of some rare World War 2 colour photographs, now believed to be held in the RAF Museum collection. The use of the locomotive's name in this way ensured that the fame of *Flying Scotsman* reached new heights.

RECLASSIFYING AND RENUMBERING

Gresley's 'A1' class Pacifics were progressively being upgraded to 'A3' class, with higher pressure boilers and numerous other detail modifications to increase power and efficiency. Nevertheless both types were used side by side and no particular urgency appears to have been given to the rebuilds, the first being dealt with in July 1927 but the last not until December 1948, nearly a year after Nationalisation of the railways. Gresley's successor, Edward Thompson, wanted to make his own mark on express locomotive design and had taken Gresley's original Pacific, *Great Northern*, and rebuilt it making some drastic alterations. In fact, very few parts from the original locomotive were used. This was always a controversial move and it has often been asked why that particular engine was selected for such treatment. Even before the deed was done senior members of the LNER locomotive department who had worked with Gresley tried to persuade Thompson to use any of the remaining 'A1s', but not Gresley's first masterpiece. Thompson wanted to emphasise the importance of his design and when it re-emerged from Doncaster Works in September 1945 it was again classified 'A1'. The existing Gresley 'A1s' not yet upgraded to 'A3', of which No 4472 was one, had been 'downgraded' to Class A10 the previous April.

Thompson instigated a renumbering scheme in January 1946 and No 4472, erstwhile No 1472, took on the unfamiliar designation, No 502. However, within a couple of months another new numbering scheme was introduced and the Gresley Pacifics were allotted the numbers 1 to 112 with *Flying Scotsman* becoming No 103 on 5 May. Later, as British Railways 60103, this would become a locomotive number nearly as well known to enthusiasts as 4472.

UPGRADE TO CLASS A3

The programme to modify the 'A1' locomotives to 'A3' finally caught up with *Flying Scotsman* in 1946 when it entered Doncaster Works on 18 November. The first of the original 'A1' class locomotives to be upgraded with a higher pressure boiler (220psi rather than 180psi) in 1927, had been No 4480 *Enterprise,* while the last to be converted in December 1948, was No 60068 *Sir Visto.*

The easiest way to distinguish an 'A3' locomotive from an 'A1/A10' is by the square cover plate on the top sides of the smokebox of the former. This was necessary as the ends of the superheater were wider than before and protruded through the smokebox slightly. The boiler given to *Flying Scotsman* at this time was not new and had previously been carried by No 2576 *The White Knight.* Steam locomotives often had boilers swapped around or replaced, along with other important components, and for this reason a locomotive's identity is traditionally, but not always it seems, that of its main frames. As far as is known, the frames carried today by *Flying Scotsman* are the 'genuine article' of No 1472 as built in 1923, but it is not unknown for even this major feature to be replaced at some time in a locomotive's life so that in effect *nothing* of the original survives! (Roland Kennington has recently made comment on this. See Chapter 7.)

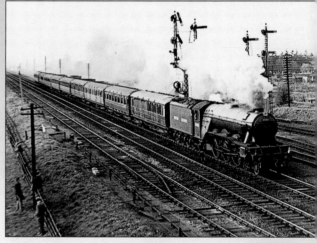

The 1946 rebuild and general repair of No 103 at this time was to be her most thorough when in main line service and it was not until 1996 that she was to be so stripped down again. The engine re-entered traffic on 4 January 1947 carrying LNER apple green livery.

REBOILERING AND RENUMBERING AGAIN

In 1948 the New Year was welcomed in by a chorus of locomotive whistles throughout the country as it was not only the end of an old year but the passing of the 'Big Four' railway companies, replaced by the Nationalised system of British Railways and a new era.

A couple of months into the new railway age and No 103 returned to Doncaster for another general repair. During the course of this overhaul a replacement boiler was fitted, this time coming from No 2505 *Cameronian*. This is worthy of comment as it brought the distinctive banjo-shaped steam dome to *Flying Scotsman* for the first time. When the locomotive re-appeared from the works on 15 March a slightly amended number was carried — E103 — the prefix denoting the Eastern Region, which included much of the former LNER network. The now-familiar BR five-figure numbering system was introduced a few months later and it was not until year's end that *Flying Scotsman* received its final BR number, carried until withdrawal in early 1963 — 60103.

A NEW COLOUR AND A CHANGE OF SCENE

Just as it took the newly Nationalised railway a while to sort out its locomotive numbering system, so it was with liveries. Railway colour schemes are always an emotive issue, and over the years it has been one of the most aired of subjects in the letters pages of the railway press. In pre-privatisation days there was inevitably disgruntled correspondence whenever a new livery was introduced, just as there was when it was later phased out, but today there are so many liveries coming and going the correspondents can't keep up! As will be seen later, *Flying Scotsman* was to be the butt of more criticism on the topic of its livery than any other individual locomotive in history when, in the 1990s, it reverted to an earlier style. However, at the time of Natonalisation it was railway executives and the travelling public, rather than enthusiasts, who were concerned about the appearance of the 'new' railway. Various experimental liveries were tried on selected locomotives and rolling stock, and differing views expressed. Eventually it was decided that main line express engines would be painted blue, lined black and white and all the 'A3s' except two received this livery. No 60103 was outshopped in blue on 16 December 1949 but this was to be a short-lived style as from August 1951 the standard livery for passenger engines was changed to the GWR's Brunswick green with black and orange lining. *Flying Scotsman* first

Opposite:
The already well-known number, 4472, was lost in 1946, first being replaced by 502 in January then 103 in May. Photographed carrying this identity on an 'up' express in late LNER days, this too was changed a couple of years later following Nationalisation in 1948. First to E103, then to 60103, which subsequently also became a famous number.
R. F. Dearden/Ian Allan Library

Opposite inset:
No 60103 heads an up relief Leeds-King's Cross working as it approaches Retford in 1948. The locomotive is in apple green livery with the tender lettered 'British Railways'. *Eric Oldham*

Below:
On Great Central metals, No 60103 blackens the skies on 28 February 1953 at Manchester London Road station. *Eric Oldham/Ian Allan Library*

appeared in this livery on 14 March 1952. Brunswick green was to remain in vogue until the end of steam traction on BR in 1968 and has been seen on this locomotive since then, but so far the blue livery has not been carried again.

Certain liveries suit some locomotives better than others. The blue looked particularly smart on Gresley's 'A4' class streamlined Pacifics and this colour scheme has been seen in recent years for the first time since the early 1950s, when it was applied to the preserved No 60007 *Sir Nigel Gresley*. However, you do not have to *see* a Great Western 'King' class 4-6-0 in blue to know that this is not *their* colour.

Whilst in its blue livery No 60103 also underwent a change of operating area when, on 4 June 1950 a transfer was made to the Eastern Region depot at Leicester. This was not its first time on the old Great Central lines; after all, its public debut in 1923 had been at Marylebone station in London, and four months had been spent based at Gorton depot, Manchester in 1944, but this was to be its longest spell away from the East Coast main line. It was not until November 1953 that *Flying Scotsman* was back on the old Great Northern when transferred to Grantham depot.

Inset:
A special working for the Westminster Bank Railway Society at York on 16 April 1955 — and still with single chimney. *Ian Allan Library*

No 60103 at its home shed of 36A Doncaster on 23 May 1959. At this stage, it was fitted with a double blastpipe and chimney but not yet equipped with the German-style smoke deflectors. *Brian Morrison*

ROUTINE DUTIES AND FOREIGN APPENDAGES

The time spent on the Great Central shows that by then this locomotive was regarded by the operating department as simply being one of, and no different from, the other 77 'A3' Pacifics. Despite its name it rarely, if ever, managed to work north of the Border, its work being confined to the southern section of the East Coast main line even when allocated for use on that route. Its claims to fame were not entirely forgotten, however, and although rail tours were not quite so common in the 1950s as later, organisers occasionally requested *Flying Scotsman*.

The 'A3s' were no longer working the crack expresses but they were still considered useful locomotives and it was known that their performance and economy could be improved if they were fitted with Kylchap double blastpipe and chimney. The use of this equipment was strongly advocated by a certain part-time member of the Eastern Area Board of the British Transport Commission despite the fact that the locomotives were obviously nearing the end of their long and successful working lives. It was argued that the cost of installation would be more than off-set by the savings made during their remaining years. This chimney arrangement made an obvious visual difference to the locomotive and, perhaps ironically, it was their proponent, Alan Pegler, who later insisted on its removal and refitting of a single chimney — for aesthetic reasons — when he bought *Flying Scotsman*. But what was uppermost in his mind when suggesting the Kylchap — saving BR some finance, or ensuring the 'A3s' might continue in traffic a little longer? Either way, the decision was clearly in the national interest... It was not a new idea by any means though, and as far back as 1937, No 2751 *Humorist* had been so equipped. The system dated back to 1919 when the Finnish engineer, Kylälä, had invented a device to improve the exhaust of gas and steam and which had in turn been developed by the eminent French engineer, André Chapelon, hence the term 'Kylchap'. So often, *Flying Scotsman* seems to have undergone change at year's end and so it was that its new chimney and blastpipe were installed during December 1958 and it re-entered traffic in this new guise the following month, the work having cost all of £153.

As successful as this new exhaust arrangement was, and it had been well proven on the 'A4' Pacifics, the non-streamlined engines were then found to suffer from problems caused by smoke and steam drifting down and along the sides of the locomotive and thus obscuring the crew's view ahead. After some experimentation it was found that the best solution was to affix German-style smoke deflectors to the sides of the smokebox, thus completing the 'internationalisation' of the front end of these otherwise very British-looking locomotives. There is always the potential problem that smoke deflectors, which assist the exhaust to rise up and over the top of the engine, do themselves obstruct the forward view. These rather unattractive accoutrements may have been effective and distinctive on the 'A3s' but they cannot really be said to have made the engines any more handsome than they already were. No 60103 did not receive its smoke deflectors until December 1961 and this was to be its final modification in appearance until withdrawn from traffic, just over a year later.

SAVE OUR SCOTSMAN

In the early 1960s railway preservation was almost entirely in the hands of the British Transport Commission which it was considered had a certain moral obligation to retain what were described as historical 'relics' for the future. The main collection of locomotives was at York where a railway museum had been established by the LNER which included a representative range of East Coast main line locomotives from the Great Northern and North Eastern railways. The other important collection was at the Science Museum, South Kensington where several early locomotives were kept, such as the remains of Stephenson's *Rocket* — perhaps the only other challenger for the title of 'the world's most famous locomotive'. This and the working, full-size replica of *Rocket* are the only other locomotives that have travelled the world anything like as much as *Flying Scotsman*, but being considerably smaller and lighter, much of their mileage has been by air!

Following a great deal of anticipation, a list of locomotives that would be spared from scrapping was announced by the BTC in early 1961. Much of the selection was made by the 'Consultative Panel' which included representatives from the principal railway and historical societies of the day that had advised the BTC's Curator of Historical Relics. Publication of news items in the railway press was not given anything like the importance or urgency of today. The list, which even varied from magazine to magazine, seems to have appeared first in the March issue of *The Railway Magazine*, then in the April *Trains Illustrated* and was not featured in *Railway World* until July, and then without any editorial comment. This certainly demonstrates just how much better served we are today by the railway press! The average enthusiast of the time, however, was no doubt more interested in what was going to happen to steam in the future than were magazine editors and the list was a major point for discussion and argument wherever they gathered, in clubs, on platforms or, as I remember, in the school playground.

It was not what was included that caused debate but what was omitted. While the Southern Railway appeared to be admirably covered by the proposed retention of a 'King Arthur', a 'Lord Nelson', a 'Schools' and a 'West Country', the LNER passenger fleet was to be represented by a 'V2' class 2-6-2, and of course, the speed record holder, *Mallard*. Even the BR Standard classes were to include not only No 70000 *Britannia* but also No 71000 *Duke of Gloucester*. Any such list was bound to be controversial, but the omission of an LMS 'Royal Scot' was surely an oversight, while the exclusion of one of Gresley's masterpieces, the 'A3s', was criminal! (The condemning of all the Peppercorn 'A1s' was also an unforgivable act, so much so that something has thankfully been done about it — hence the construction of No 60163 *Tornado*, more than 35 years later.)

The omission of an 'A3' in itself was bad enough but the record breaking *Flying Scotsman* and *Papyrus* were surely both worth saving. However, as only one of each type could then be considered, the LNER's pioneer 100mph locomotive was the obvious candidate. The official reason for not including the 'A3' was two fold. First, there was a place for only one Gresley Pacific so this had to be *Mallard*, and as an 'A3' *Flying Scotsman* was no longer in 'as-built' condition. On the other hand, the unique collection of East Coast main line motive power at York, from Stirling's 8ft single-wheeler No 1, would now have a serious gap between the Ivatt Atlantics (two) and the 'A4'.

In the event, not all the locomotives on the published list were actually saved officially and it was left to private finance, and determination, to secure No 71000 and a BR Standard Class 5 with Caprotti valve gear, for instance.

Although the railway press was dismissive of the importance or degree of interest in preservation at the time, the correspondence pages soon began to show that readers did care about such things. The very next issue of *The Railway Magazine* carried a letter from a Mr Walford of Devon pointing out some of the anomalies of the official list and in particular, the obvious omission of *Flying Scotsman*.

The final BR guise — Brunswick green livery, double chimney and the distinctive German-style smoke deflectors. This is the occasion of its official 'last run' in Nationalised ownership on 14 January 1963 and with snow on the ground makes a spectacular sight as it leaves Peterborough North with the 13.15 King's Cross to Leeds.
J. C. Haydon/Ian Allan Library

The number of locomotives that it appeared would be surviving at that time was unquestionably minimal, bearing in mind that upon Nationalisation BR had inherited just over 20,000 — yes twenty-thousand — steam locomotives of more than 400 different types. Space to store preserved locomotives was needless to say an oft-quoted reason for keeping the numbers down, but it is difficult to equate this with the amount of land and buildings that were about to become surplus to requirements and still to be owned by the British Railways Board. Many large engine sheds were to remain empty but intact on railway-owned land, some right through to the present day. Also, acres of land from old goods yards and miles of disused trackbed stood unused, much of it to the end of the century and possibly beyond as it turned out, so to say that there was *nowhere* to store another few historically important locomotives and items of rolling stock is difficult to accept.

Public display of these 'relics' was not considered a high priority at this time in any case as many of the officially preserved locomotives were already stored at locations not readily accessible to the general public. And of course, it was static display that was regarded as the correct and proper course of action, or rather inaction. A number of narrow gauge railways were being revitalised in North and Mid Wales and the Bluebell and Middleton railways had commenced operations with small tank engines, but there was absolutely no intention that the 'National Collection' locomotives should ever be seen in steam again. Therefore, any disused building large enough could have been used to store historic locomotives, rather than cut them up.

Clearly, railway preservation was in its infancy although this was not necessarily obvious at the time as a few static exhibits and a couple of truncated branch lines did not exactly constitute a 'movement' or much indication of the future good health of steam railways. A number of appeals for locomotives were being launched and announced in the railway press, but in nearly every case, the magazines devoted as much space to correspondence condemning or criticising the proposals, making for much depressing and discouraging reading.

By early 1962 a handful of 'A3s' had already been withdrawn and condemned to scrap and it was evident that for the rest of the class their days were numbered. The March issue of *The Railway Magazine* carried a letter from a Mr R. A. Ferguson of Edinburgh announcing the existence of the Gresley 'A3' Preservation Society which had been formed the previous autumn. It stated that the society had nearly 50 members and this would have to be increased if they were to succeed, as the scrap price asked by BR for an 'A3' was £3,000. An all-out effort was being made to recruit new members. It was realised that the number of organisations appealing for money and members was nearly as numerous as there were locomotive classes, but correspondence with the Railway Preservation Society had elicited the fact that while they could not help the project financially, they did at least 'condone' the proposal. (That was jolly good of them!) The letter ended with the statement that 'all our members deplore the fact that an "A3" is not earmarked for preservation, and our sole aim is to rectify this state of affairs'.

The October issue of the magazine carried a brief, small advertisement, again from Mr Ferguson: 'SAVE OUR SCOTSMAN! Enthusiasts, help save the famous historic Pacific locomotive *Flying Scotsman* by joining the Gresley "A3" Preservation Society. Details from the Hon Secretary...'

The Society's target had now been identified! It appears that the first time this project actually reached the news pages of the magazine was just before Christmas 1962, in the issue dated January 1963. This read: 'Mr B. Rowe, Advertising & Publicity Manager of the Gresley "A3" Preservation Society, reports that although the Society has been in existence for just over twelve months and is showing steady growth, the membership is still only approximately 300 and more are needed. There is no age limit and no fixed membership fee, and readers who are interested and anxious to assist in the effort to preserve an "A3" Pacific should address a letter to the Hon Secretary, Mr Ramsay Ferguson, Edinburgh...'

Time was running out for the 'A3s' — and *Flying Scotsman* in particular. On 14 January it worked the 1.15pm King's Cross as far as Doncaster. The next day it was officially withdrawn from BR traffic. No 60103 *Flying Scotsman*, Doncaster Works No 1564 was exactly 40 years old and had come to the end of the line, and was credited with having run a total of 2,076,000 miles.

2 LIFE BEGINS AT 40

In late 1962 the railway scene was vastly different to today. There was still a great deal of steam traction at work on British Railways, and although its planned abolition before the decade was out had been made well known, it was difficult to imagine that after nearly 140 years the so-called modern traction would take over entirely. Many of the diesels then being introduced were proving to be less than successful and the occasions when a steam locomotive was summoned to rescue a breakdown were far from rare.

Many people were working towards saving representative members of different classes of locomotive and a number of schemes to preserve branch lines were gathering momentum. The idea that a locomotive could be purchased and then run on the BR *main* line was but a pipe dream for most. However, there are always people who have a vision shared with determination and enthusiasm and, if fortunate enough, the financial means to achieve what others say is impossible. One such man was Alan Pegler of Doncaster.

Even today, the name Alan Pegler is synonymous with, and therefore virtually as well known as, *Flying Scotsman*, the locomotive he bought in 1963. He continues to be associated with the locomotive as he is now Honorary President of the supporters' organisation, the Flying Scotsman Association. The locomotive has changed hands several times since he secured it from BR, but it is this first private owner who will forever be linked with the name *Flying Scotsman* — and this is not the result of chance. Alan Pegler was already a well-known name in railway circles and if anyone was going to move railway preservation up a gear, then it was no suprise that it was he. Alan was known not only for being an organiser of successful rail tours when such events were a rarity, but he had also bought a railway!

A RAILWAY OF HIS OWN

A group of railway enthusiasts, inspired by the successful acquisition and operation of the narrow gauge Talyllyn Railway, were trying to buy the closed and derelict Festiniog Railway but were finding the tangle of legal problems too difficult to unravel. In fact, initially, it was this railway that three Midlands' friends had aimed to run as the first volunteer operated railway. But, for various reasons, not least the problem of the company's creditors, they had been persuaded to look elsewhere, and hence the historic volunteer takeover of the Talyllyn in 1950. There was only one way forward for the FR and that was for a block of shares to be purchased in order to give a controlling interest and thus allow restoration to proceed. The young Alan Pegler was most enthusiastic about the project, greatly encouraged by an old friend, Trevor Bailey. Negotiations eventually reached the stage where sufficient shares were available and that appeared to offer a once-in-a-lifetime opportunity to save the historic Festiniog Railway. However, the amount required was £3,000, a huge sum for railway enthusiasts to find in the early 1950s. Alan Pegler however, was in a sufficiently healthy financial position to be able to obtain a bank loan to buy the shares. At this point, Alan's father stepped in with an interest-free loan to his son to avoid him being saddled with bank interest charges. Alan then bought the shares and immediately became the proud owner of a completely derelict narrow gauge railway in North Wales!

Alan realised that if he remained owner then it would always be *his* railway and it would never be easy to persuade people to give up their time and energies on a voluntary basis. Therefore, the very next day, the shares were vested in the Festiniog Railway Trust which to this day, owns the railway which is one of the most popular and successful steam railways in the world. Alan Pegler did not become a trustee but has the unique position of being the person who alone appoints the trustees, of whom there are always five. He is still closely connected with the railway and is its greatest ambassador wherever he goes.

GREAT NORTHERN RAIL TOURS

As important a step in railway preservation as it was, acquiring the Festiniog was perhaps not quite so beneficial an experience to the success of the later *Flying Scotsman* venture as Alan's other activity as an organiser of rail tours. In 1950, Alan had travelled on a special train on the East Coast main line from King's Cross to mark the passing of the Ivatt Atlantics and, inspired by this occasion, he decided to organise a train himself the following year. This ran from Retford to King's Cross to mark the 80th anniversary of the Northern Rubber Company and the motive power chosen was No 60113 *Great Northern*, the Thompson rebuild of the original Gresley Pacific. The following year saw the 'Centenaries Express', powered by an 'A4' class Pacific and, in 1953, a hundred years of Doncaster Works was commemorated with the 'Plant Centenarian'. This was worked by the two preserved Great Northern Railway Atlantics. Thereafter, Alan made all the arrangements for two specials each year, one of which was always for Northern Rubber, right up to the time that he left the company in 1961. The trains became more and more ambitious in their routing and choice of motive power and each tour was a real occasion.

Alan Pegler was appointed to the Eastern Area Board of the British Transport Commission in 1955. He was pleased to learn on joining the Board, that he had the authority to travel on the footplate of ER locomotives whenever he wished. Taking advantage of this privilege he soon became well acquainted with the top link drivers on the East Coast main line. This was not just as a passenger either, as he would more often than not take the shovel and keep the fire in shape!

A LOCOMOTIVE OF HIS OWN

Alan Pegler had always favoured Gresley's unstreamlined Pacifics in preference to the 'A4s' and one locomotive in particular — the very first he had seen as the small boy at the beginning of this story at the exhibition in Wembley — *Flying Scotsman*. The fact that 'his' engine had subsequently obtained a certain degree of fame and prestige was really incidental to Alan's love of the engine, although it was rather satisfying to have sensed such charisma when so young. It was while attending the annual dinner of the Gainsborough Model Railway Society that Alan was asked if he might be prepared to contribute to a locomotive fund which it was thought might interest him. This was in support of the Save Our Scotsman fund. However, Alan tactfully declined but said he would think about it. The reason for his reluctance was that only a few days earlier he had entered into negotiations for a deal with British Railways to buy the locomotive, but it was not yet at a stage to make a public announcement.

The choice of *Flying Scotsman* for preservation was clearly a good one on a number of accounts. The prime reason, however, as far as Alan was concerned, was that it was his personal favourite locomotive, dating back to that first encounter at Wembley. Secondly, it represented one of the most important classes of locomotive in British railway history, and none of the Gresley 'A1/A3s' was otherwise going to be saved for posterity. This was quite a remarkable omission from the National Collection and had this one not been saved then it could well be that today, instead of a *Peppercorn* 'A1' class being built as a full-size, working replica, it would be a *Gresley* Pacific now under construction. Indeed, in view of the immense worldwide popularity of *Flying Scotsman* today it could perhaps be argued that a second one might in fact be more commercially viable to build new rather than any other type of extinct locomotive! Finished in LNER apple green, perhaps as No 1472 instead of No 60103 in dark Brunswick green, it might even have stolen some of the limelight. It is amusing to recall that when *Flying Scotsman*, as No 60103, arrived at the Swanage Railway in 1995 rumours abounded in the Southwest that the locomotive the railway had received and was publicising was not the *real Flying Scotsman* despite the nameplates carried, as it did not look as expected — it was the wrong colour and did not have the right number! More recently, again on the Swanage Railway, Bulleid Pacific No 34072 *257 Squadron* took on the identity of No 34023 *Blackmoor Vale* when the occasion demanded, even though that locomotive is in existence and kept elsewhere. With celebrity lookalikes so common these days, making 'official' appearances, a second *Flying Scotsman* would probably not be one too many for the world today...

As a businessman, Alan Pegler always saw his locomotive as a commercial venture and what better name for it to carry than that of the world's most famous *train*. Most people don't know the difference between a 'train' and a 'locomotive' — hence the term 'trainspotter' — and so he had an immediate marketing benefit to be exploited.

THE LAST RUN

The locomotive did not actually change hands until 16 April 1963 but the public announcement of the acquisition coincided with its last revenue-earning run on British Railways on 14 January. A public relations company was employed to ensure maximum publicity, a course of action perhaps not so common then as today. The company was instructed to ensure that *all* references to the locomotive should contain two elements — 1) that it was now owned by Mr Alan Pegler and 2) that it was 'the world's most famous locomotive'. With no other contenders for the title, *Flying Scotsman* had a clear road ahead to fame, if not fortune. Professional publicity was employed until spring 1968, by which time it was not felt necessary — the locomotive no longer needed any help in attracting media attention.

The media seized on the publicity immediately it was released. Here was a fantastic story, a charismatic railway enthusiast who had just bought his very own giant steam locomotive with the intention of keeping it running on the main line, even after BR had got rid of all theirs. This was a real David and Goliath situation, the lone enthusiast taking on a nationalised industry. In January 1963, Britain was in the grip of a big freeze and on the morning of the 14, King's Cross 'Top Shed' seemed like the coldest place on Earth. No 60103 was being prepared for its last duty on BR, the 1.15pm King's Cross to Leeds, working as far as Doncaster. Despite the conditions the press and television people turned out in force and were given access to 'Top Shed', where Alan Pegler was on hand to explain what was happening. This was international news and the press included representatives from the USA and Canada.

Due to the advance publicity large crowds had gathered at King's Cross station and the stationmaster, complete with top hat — traditional dress for big occasions at the station — was in attendance and read out messages of congratulations to Alan Pegler and the footplate crew, all of whom were wearing carnations. Alan's wife Pauline was there to travel in the train, while her husband had on his overalls in readiness for a trip on the footplate. The train pulled out majestically from the station and, dead on time, passed the large signalbox and headed northwards into the smoky gloom of Gasworks Tunnel. Although the locomotive's future was now assured, it was nevertheless a sad occasion, as it was another step towards the end of an era. Steam locomotives had set off from this station daily since 14 October 1852. All along the route railwaymen and enthusiasts were gathered in large numbers to cheer the train on as it pounded its way through the snow-covered landscape, each knowing it was a historic moment in railway history. They may have seen similar locomotives on this route countless times before, but this really was a sight never to forget.

The end of one era, and the beginning of another. No 60103 made its farewell appearance in BR service on 14 January 1963 but its future had already been secured by Alan Pegler. It was an occasion tinged with sadness but the announcement that it had been saved from the cutter's torch was cause for celebration. *Ian Allan Library*

While passengers were enjoying their lunch in relaxed comfort, the train reached its maximum speed of 90mph on this historic journey. After a quick stop had been made at Peterborough, Retford — 138 miles from the capital — was reached with 4 minutes to spare. The train approached Doncaster just as the sun was setting in a frosty sky, the arrival being timed at 6 minutes ahead of schedule. Here, No 60103 was taken off the train to start a new life, and as it transpired, an even more exciting and adventurous career than it had enjoyed in its first 40 years of existence. Alan Pegler remarked that he did not have a 'collector's' instinct and was a selective buyer. After all, he had only ever bought two items of note: one was the world's best railway and the other the world's finest locomotive...

'FLYING SCOTSMAN' IS SAVED

This was the heading in the February 1963 issue of *The Railway Magazine* announcing that the locomotive had been rescued from destruction by a businessman for £3,000. It is interesting to look back at how the railway press of the day treated such a momentous news item. Today, there are a number of magazines packed full of railway preservation news items, all vying to have the story out first with front covers screaming out the latest 'scoop' and with bold headlines inside drawing attention to the most recent developments, all illustrated with colour photographs, some barely a week old when the magazine reaches the news stands. It was all so very different in 1963. Preservation was not really regarded as being serious 'railway' by the magazines of the day and preservation schemes, including the successful ones, were looked upon as novelty items, news stories appearing as and when space from 'proper' railway news allowed.

It was probably the acquisition of *Flying Scotsman* for main line running that was the start of the new era as much as anything, but the significance was not detected at the time. The above mentioned report appeared on the second of the news pages in the magazine and was no more than about 150 words, with no picture. The 14 January run was mentioned along with the fact that whilst it was a sad day for many 'at least it was not heading for the scrap heap'. The editor was clearly able to contain his excitement about the prospect of the locomotive entertaining millions worldwide in the years to come. The March issue however, featured an uncaptioned illustration of No 60103 on the cover as well as another view, also in black and white of course, as a frontispiece.

The other main railway news magazine of the day, *Modern Railways*, was happy to wait until the March issue before broadcasting this major story, but did include a BR photograph of the locomotive at King's Cross before setting off with the 1.15pm on that historic day. The news itself did not warrant a headline or a separate item, appearing in the 'Motive Power Miscellany' section under 'Eastern Region' where the fact that 'A3 class 4-6-2 No 60103 has been purchased for restoration and hiring out for occasional special trains' appeared between the news that Classes K3 and L1 had been rendered extinct by the latest withdrawals and that King's Cross and Grantham steam depots were to close later in the year. The national media on the other hand, had responded far more positively and had seen the potential public interest in such a venture.

PREPARATIONS FOR A NEW CAREER

As soon as *Flying Scotsman* came off the train at Doncaster it made its way to the place of its birth, the 'Plant' (Doncaster Works), where restoration in accordance with its new owner's wishes was to take place. The basic aim was to restore the locomotive to how it would have been in LNER days, but there was no question of un-rebuilding it to 'A1' status. The compromise was to replace its double chimney with a single enabling the German-style smoke deflectors to be discarded, and LNER apple green livery with the locomotive's best-known number, 4472. The ever-critical enthusiasts were quick to point out that as an 'A3' it had never been in apple green with this number, so it was 'unauthentic'. This ignored a certain number of basic facts such as the new owner was not making a historical model — this was the *real* thing! He had the right to paint it whatever colour he pleased, just as the previous owners had — other than BR Brunswick green as at that time this was still the standard livery of locomotives owned by the nationalised rail network. Furthermore, that was how he *wanted* it to look; it was not down to ignorance, as who else knew more about Gresley's non-streamlined Pacifics than Alan Pegler?

It was the finishing touch that also brought further criticism from certain quarters — the red background to the nameplate. But how smart and distinctive it looks when you see the result in colour photographs, compared with the nondescript black used before and since, and as mentioned previously, this had been one of Gresley's ideas. According to Alf Parsons of the Doncaster paintshop this was definitely proposed for some engines, but never implemented, until now. The locomotive had the red-backed nameplate all the time it was in Alan Pegler's ownership, and at no other time, so it is a useful identification feature when seen in photographs.

A RETURN TO STEAM

Just 24 days after arriving from London, *Flying Scotsman* was ready for its steam trials, following restoration to single-chimney status. Two trial runs were made to New England and back, its appearance on these journeys being unique. The smoke deflectors were gone, the oval brass builder's plates had been moved from the cab side, back to the side of the smokebox as originally fitted and the BR smokebox number plate had been removed, but the locomotive remained in its Brunswick green livery with 60103 on the cab side and BR emblem on the tender. The speed was restricted to 60mph on these occasions because of the effects of adverse weather on the tracks, but the trials were nevertheless a success.

As an aside, the smokebox number plate that had been removed was, many years later, not only the subject of bigger headlines in the railway press than the original purchase of the locomotive, but was sold for a greater figure! The 60103 smokebox number plate was retained by Alan Pegler for many years and mounted on a polished wood background with its BR 34A (King's Cross) shed code plate. It had to be sold in the early 1970s when finances were not too good following the American saga, described later. Then, in July 1996, this item came up for sale again by auction and was sold to a private collector in the south of England for £4,350, a record sum for such a plate.

On 26 March 1963 the locomotive emerged from the paintshop at Doncaster following the completion of its restoration, resplendent in LNER apple green livery and carrying the number 4472 in gold leaf on the cab side. It now had a corridor tender again, this having previously been coupled to 'A4' Pacific No 60034 *Lord Faringdon*. This roll-out was unpublicised and was witnessed only by Alan and Pauline Pegler with a few railway officials, but fortunately the event was captured on cine film. Also without publicity was a run three days later to Barkston and back, working light. Barkston, situated north of Grantham on the East Coast main line, had lost its station in 1955 but had become a regular destination for locomotives on running-in trips from Doncaster Works following completion of building or repair. In 1938, *Mallard* had made this journey immediately prior to her world record breaking run.

Flying Scotsman hauled a two-coach train, again without publicity, in early April, working up to Finsbury Park, London travelling via Lincoln, March and Cambridge. This was all in preparation for its first appearance in public since acquisition for preservation.

Carrying train reporting number X28, the first privately owned steam locomotive to work on Britain's main line heads its inaugural train which took place on 20 April 1963, only four days after formal purchase by Alan Pegler. This was run in connection with the Festiniog Railways' cententary of steam celebrations, working the excursion from Paddington to Ruabon and is seen here passing through Ardley. *G. T. Robinson/Ian Allan Library*

A NEW LEASE OF LIFE

The transfer of ownership of the locomotive was recorded as being 16 April 1963, the deal including the exclusive use of an old engine weigh-house at Doncaster as an operating base and a three-year running agreement on the national rail network, expiring in mid-April 1966. When this news reached the then Chairman of BR, the infamous Dr Beeching, he was said to be 'not best pleased'. He certainly did not think it fitting that a member of the Board, part time or otherwise, should own and run his own locomotive. Probably not for the last time in railway preservation history, an enthusiast was given the choice, 'it's the loco or me', but more usually the threat comes from a spouse. Again, as has often been the case, there was no contest. The running agreement was later extended for a further five years to April 1971, well beyond the demise of BR's steam fleet. This move turned out to be very wise and significant on Alan Pegler's part. At the time of purchase it was agreed that the new owner would not be allowed to drive the locomotive, this condition being at the insistence of the unions, but he would be permitted to travel on the footplate and generally make himself 'useful'.

The first public outing took place only four days after the change of ownership, on 20 April 1963. This train was well publicised with all seats sold several weeks in advance. Combining Alan Pegler's various railway interests, the rail tour was for the Festiniog Railway Society, who were commemorating the centenary of steam on the narrow gauge railway. The intention, right from the start, was to spread the word of *Flying Scotsman*, by traversing tracks and heading for destinations that had never seen a Gresley Pacific before. It was therefore appropriate for No 4472 to go west from the old Great Western terminus of Paddington which, when built, was situated so far from the centre of London that cynics had joked, 'Paddington, change here for London', but the GWR had had the last laugh — London had extended westwards to meet it!

This historic special — the first main line excursion to be headed by a privately owned steam locomotive — ran to Ruabon, taking the locomotive into the Principality of Wales for the first time ever. The Pacific carried the Western-style headcode 'X28' on its smokebox and attracted huge crowds to witness the departure, despite appalling weather — heavy rain and strong winds. The conditions did not dampen the spirits of enthusiasts in the Midlands either and a crowd, stated to be in the region of 8,000 people, lined the platforms (and the tracks well beyond) at Birmingham Snow Hill where the train stopped for water, and experienced some delay. Arrival at Ruabon was again greeted by large crowds, who saw the locomotive detach from the train and head off light to Shrewsbury, in order to work the special back to London from there later in the day.

The second public duty for the preserved *Flying Scotsman* took it to the South Coast, another part of the country never visited before, other than perhaps in the minds of those prewar postcard manufacturers! Organised by the Gainsborough Model Railway Society, of which Alan Pegler was President, the train was a most unusual working, starting at Lincoln and travelling via Nottingham, Leicester and Oxford to Southampton, with locomotive servicing taking place at Eastleigh depot. The return journey was more than 500 miles and was worked without any mechanical problems, and once again, all seats were sold well in advance.

These two trips had been 'flag waving' exercises to prove the commercial viability of such excursions, as well as the operational feasibility. Today, long-distance steam operations by privately owned locomotives are taken for granted, but in the early 1960s it all had to be proved, and Alan Pegler and *Flying Scotsman* not only showed what could be done, but also how.

MAIN LINE OPERATIONS

For over 30 years this famous locomotive plied the tracks of British Rail, barring a couple of breaks for overseas holidays, clocking up something like 340,000 miles on UK tracks alone. For the rest of 1964 it was a regular sight on excursions throughout the network with each train working to a new destination, or

On 18 March 1964 a three-coach special was worked from Doncaster to Cardiff, via Sheffield, Derby and Gloucester. This was to take Alan Pegler to receive an award from the Wales Tourist Board for 'services to tourism in Wales' through his role as Chairman of the Festiniog Railway. A spirited departure is made from Gloucester Central. *B. J. Ashworth/Ian Allan Library*

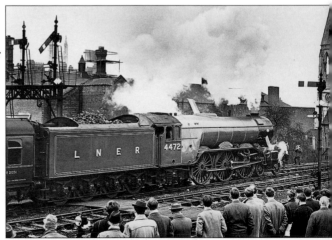

some other notable 'first' being added to the locomotive's story. These travels would easily fill a book in themselves but here, only the major landmarks can be recounted.

On 18 April, for example, the 'Great Central Rail Tour' was worked from Manchester to London Marylebone via the Woodhead route and was the first steam-hauled train for 10 years through the notorious Woodhead Tunnel which is over three miles in length. At first, the idea was given the thumbs down as the tunnel had been relined at the time of electrification. It was considered that there was now insufficient ventilation for a steam locomotive and that the new lining was not sulphur-resistant. It was then pointed out that in Belgium, where a similar situation existed, steam locomotives were hauled through the tunnel, in steam, by an electric locomotive and all was well. This was agreed for this occasion and so *Flying Scotsman* made a unique passage through this tunnel which was on a route that has since been closed to all traffic. The tunnel still sees occasional rail use though as the National Grid has a 2ft gauge railway with diesel and electric locomotives which is used for maintenance purposes in connection with the power cables that now pass through the tunnel.

Left:
Flying Scotsman had to be escorted through Woodhead Tunnel by electric locomotive (No 26001) while working the Great Central Rail Tour as steam was normally prohibited from that route.
Gavin Morrison

Below:
A month later the ground-breaking Great Central Rail Tour was run (18 April) with a stop at Leicester South Goods for a crew change and water.
Colin P. Walker/Ian Allan Library

The following month No 4472 was to work a historic and memorable train to Scotland — claimed to be its first crossing of the Border, despite its name, for a remarkable 25 years! This just had to be a special occasion, so Alan Pegler hired the entire train of Pullman cars normally used on the 'Master Cutler'. The train was named 'Pegler's Pullman' and ran from Doncaster to Edinburgh Waverley where an official welcome was laid on. *Flying Scotsman* did not head the train back that day as it was to have a short stay in Scotland.

A classic view later made famous by Terence Cuneo's painting as *Flying Scotsman* crosses the Forth Bridge on 15 May 1964 on an Aberdeen working. Note the ferry, right, since replaced by the road bridge. *W. J. V. Anderson/Ian Allan Library*

A few days after arrival north of the Border the locomotive was taken to the Forth Bridge where it stopped for a while so that the late Terence Cuneo could make some sketches in preparation for a painting which has since become one of his best known works. It was later reproduced as a fine art print, limited to 850 copies, which were all signed by the artist, Sir William McAlpine and Alan Pegler, and are today valued collector's items. The original painting was sold at auction in September 1996, fetching the highest price ever paid for a Cuneo, as detailed later.

A NEW BOILER, A REPAINT AND ANOTHER RECORD

No 4472 had been in more or less constant use since acquisition by Alan Pegler and it became due for a heavy repair in November 1964. This work was undertaken at Darlington and on completion a small but obvious change in appearance had taken place. The cylinder covers, instead of being unlined black, were now painted green, edged with black and white lining; a distinctive trade mark of a locomotive receiving attention at this works. Another useful marker when dating photographs.

The 1965 season once again saw the locomotive in regular operation, on occasions reaching parts of the country that other LNER Pacifics had failed to reach before. One notable destination was Weymouth, while Cardiff proved to be more troublesome to achieve. An attempt was made on 9 October 1965 to break the speed record for steam traction on the Great Western route from London Paddington to Cardiff, perhaps to prove a point? Organised by *Railway Magazine* the 'Welsh Mystery

When first being operated in preservation it was possible to pick up water en route as water troughs still survived at certain locations such as at Wiske Moor, Northallerton. Alan Pegler gives a wave from the footplate on 10 April 1965 which was the first outing following overhaul at Darlington Works. The train used the stock of the 'Tees-Tyne Pullman' and carried about 120 men who had been engaged in the overhaul of the locomotive as a 'thank you'. *Maurice S. Burns/Ian Allan Library*

Flyer' was advertised as being a 'great day for railway enthusiasts' for a fare of only £4. After a good start from Paddington, the locomotive began showing obvious signs of ill health as the train headed west through the Wiltshire countryside. On arrival at Swindon, where a stop had been scheduled for water, the locomotive was taken off the train, which continued its journey behind a 'Hymek' diesel-hydraulic, arriving at Cardiff only 15 minutes down on time.

An immediate inspection was carried out on No 4472 to discover what had led to this very rare failure and it was soon found that the back, left-hand steam chest cover had come adrift, all eight securing nuts having come loose. This was an embarrassing incident and Alan Pegler placed the following announcement in the November issue of *Railway Magazine*:

'FOR THE BENEFIT OF DISAPPOINTED LINE-SIDE SPECTATORS, Mr Alan Pegler is running a *Flying Scotsman*-hauled private train on Saturday, November 13, to the 140min timing — Paddington dep 9.30; Cardiff ar. 11.50. It will return at 14.30 on a similar schedule.'

How the attitude of some rail tour operators has changed over the years — 'for the benefit of disappointed *line-side spectators*' he said! Perhaps this is one of the reasons why Alan Pegler will always be regarded with such great affection by enthusiasts, compared with some of his counterparts of more recent times. It was also notable that by now even the railway press appreciated the importance of this locomotive and the interest it aroused.

This second Cardiff train has gone down as possibly one of the most notable and best-remembered that *Scotsman* has worked in its preservation career. This was the 'Panda Pullman' which was organised by Alan Pegler in conjunction with Peter Scott on behalf of the World Wildlife Fund, as it was then. On both trains the locomotive carried a large circular headboard, the latter graced by a huge illustration of a giant panda. The tour brochure for the second train carried an explanation for the earlier failure which quoted the

The preserved 'A3' class Pacific rushes through Badminton station on 13 November 1965 with the 'Panda Pullman'. *Ronald E. Toop*

insurer's statement that 'the nut in question had been intentionally slackened off by some person maliciously'. So deliberate sabotage had been inflicted, no doubt by someone who did not wish to see steam being perpetuated on Britain's main lines.

The 'Panda Pullman' comprised five coaches including an observation car and, despite an extended stop of 7 minutes at Swindon for water, it arrived at Cardiff in 2hr 17min and claimed the speed record for this journey for steam traction, which stands to this day. The average speed for the 145.2 miles, disregarding the water stop, was 67.9mph and could have been even greater had BR not stipulated a maximum speed limit of 80mph for the engine. *Flying Scotsman's* reputation for faultless running and record breaking had been restored.

SERVICING THE SCOTSMAN

Enthusiastic cleaners set to work on No 4472's smokebox at Norwich MPD on 6 May 1967.
*P. Hocquard/
Ian Allan Library*

Left:
This view of the cleaning in progress at Norwich shows the square cover on the top side of the smokebox which is a distinguishing feature between Gresley 'A1' and 'A3' class Pacifics. *P. Hocquard/Ian Allan Library*

Below:
Alan Pegler, left, supervises the taking on of water at Leicester London Road station on 23 March 1968, the train being the 'Brontë Railtour'. *Graham S. Cocks/Ian Allan Library*

Even *Flying Scotsman* is dwarfed by the huge concrete coaling tower at Carnforth depot, itself a remarkable survivor, but for how much longer? 17 March 1968. *Brian Stephenson/Ian Allan Library*

TWO TENDERS *SCOTSMAN*

Running rail tours in those pioneering days of preservation had the advantage that much of the infrastructure of the steam railway was still in place. Long-distance nonstop runs were made possible by the fact that water troughs were still in situ and so the locomotive could replenish its supply without even stopping on some routes. Water columns were to be found as often as was needed, and there were active steam locomotive depots with all the facilities to hand including coaling stages or even coaling towers that made topping up the tender a simple task. Even though *Flying Scotsman* was one of a large number of steam locomotives active on British Railways, its presence, whether at a main line terminus, or an engine shed, never failed to generate great interest, not only among the general public but railwaymen too. It was clearly the star of the show wherever it went, its magnificent and immaculate apple green livery contrasting more and more with the run-down appearance of BR's workhorses.

The agenda for the complete abolition of steam traction had been drawn up and it was obvious that servicing facilities would be swept away just as soon as they were surplus to normal requirements. The agreement to continue operations after the official end of steam appeared to indicate that No 4472 could very well, in future, be the *only* steam locomotive that would be available for such duties anyway, so the idea of establishing any permanent facilities for coaling and watering could not even be considered. Although April 1971 had been set as the expiry date for main line running, Alan Pegler had no intention of throwing down the shovel at that time and even in the 1960s, had his mind set on running his 'A3' at the time of the new millennium, then some 35 or so years hence.

Problems of servicing were creeping up gradually and at first it was possible to overcome these by forming a volunteer support group, headed by George Hinchcliffe, who was the secretary of the Gainsborough Model Railway Society. The new organisation, Flying Scotsman Enterprises, worked in conjunction with various contractors who operated coal lorries and water tankers. Some on BR appreciated the significance and PR value of these trains and a liaison officer was appointed to deal directly with Alan Pegler regarding the organising of runs throughout the network, many of which were of course inter-Regional. It was vital that supplies of coal and water would be available, by whatever means, when the locomotive required them.

However, it was a problem that needed to be tackled soon as it was becoming progressively more difficult to service the locomotive as it travelled around the country. The ingenious solution was to acquire a second tender to attach to the locomotive, thus increasing its water capacity considerably. 'A4' Pacific No 60009 *Union of South Africa* was due for withdrawal and was standing out of use at

Aberdeen. Although subsequently secured for main line operations, there was no inkling of this at the time, so its corridor tender was bought from BR for less than £1,000, as it was in quite a dilapidated condition. A further £5,000 was then spent to adapt it for its new role and to bring it back up to standard for 80mph running. It was

The two tenders are seen to advantage in this rear three-quarter view as No 4472 passes Goose Hill Junction, Normanton, on the 'Scarborough Flyer', 6 April 1968.
John S. Whiteley

modified so that it carried water only (6,000gal) but retained its corridor facility. It could be used as a reserve tank, isolated from the first tender, or the cocks could be opened so that an unlimited water supply of 11,000gal was available, giving a nonstop operating range of up to 300 miles. This would be possible with a seven-coach train, while the more usual 10 to 12 coaches reduced the range to about 150 miles, nevertheless, a useful distance to achieve without the need of external supplies.

The locomotive and existing tender entered Doncaster Works in September 1966 so that they could be repainted with the new tender to make sure there was a matching green throughout the ensemble. When completed, the engine and two tenders were slowly pulled out from the paintshop by a diesel shunter. The amazing length of the combination and its gleaming paintwork was impressive indeed. What was immediately noticeable was that now, the famous number, 4472, was not on the cab side but on the side of the *second* tender in a similar style to the LNER lettering on the first. On the locomotive's cab side were square metal plates carrying the intricate LNER coat of arms.

It was not intended that both tenders should be used for every tour and the first run after repainting, on 17 September, saw the conventional set-up in operation as usual, this being on the Southern Region, working from London Victoria to Brighton and Eastleigh. There was of course a weight penalty with the two tenders and there were bridges on this route that were not passed to accept the full combination. When running with one tender the only place where the locomotive's number was carried was on the front buffer beam, not that many 'spotters' needed to be told what it was!

The first outing with both tenders was a trial run to Barkston and back on 3 October 1966, another dull and miserable day, but much of the run was captured on cine film, shot from a chasing road vehicle. Like many of the early moments of the locomotive's preservation this footage is now available on video (see Videography). This run went without a hitch and just five days later a passenger train, operated on behalf of the Gainsborough MRS, saw the public debut of the two-tender locomotive. The 'Blackpool Belle' ran from Lincoln to the Lancashire seaside resort and back, again without any problem other than the fact that on the return there was uncertainty about the water level so an unscheduled stop was made on a remote stretch of line to make a visual check. All was well and the train continued on its journey back to Lincoln.

On another occasion, however, the footplate inspector was not convinced that there was sufficient water on a return journey, so the train was stopped on the Bedford avoiding line while the locomotive was detached and continued on into the darkness hoping to find a water column, somewhere! The driver had in fact remembered where he had seen one on a station, and after topping up the tanks, they returned to the stranded train, with its 700 or so passengers, coupled up and completed the journey to London St Pancras.

LONDON TO EDINBURGH NONSTOP

The date 1 May 1968 marked the 40th anniversary of the first London to Edinburgh nonstop run by the LNER, with *Flying Scotsman* in charge on that historic occasion. This event just *had* to be commemorated by means of a repeat performance. (It was unfortunate that it was not possible to complete the restoration of the locomotive in time for the 70th anniversary of the run in 1998.) There were some on BR who were not so keen on such an idea and a surprising amount of opposition was put up in official circles. Despite this, the event was organised due to the determination of the owner, with help from the Locomotive Club of Great Britain and those on BR sympathetic to the cause. Prior publicity was cautious, but on the dot of 10am on Wednesday, 1 May, No 4472 set off from Platform 10 at King's Cross with a seven-coach train bound for Edinburgh, allowing 7½hr for the 392.7 miles.

The original proposal was that Hawker Siddeley's brand new prototype 4,000hp Co-Co diesel-electric locomotive *Kestrel* would leave King's Cross simultaneously, departing from Platform 8 with the 'Flying Scotsman' train. Then, to further celebrate the 40th anniversary, on Saturday 4 May, *Flying Scotsman* and *Kestrel* would double-head a special, departing from Edinburgh at 14.30, working to King's Cross nonstop. In the event it was the modern traction element of the programme that had to be amended so that on 1 May the 'Flying Scotsman' was worked by one of its regular diesel-electric locomotives, 'Deltic' No D9021 *Argyll & Sutherland Highlander,* which arrived at Edinburgh the best part of two hours ahead of the steam-hauled train, even though a stop had been made at Newcastle.

All eyes were on No 4472 though, and the media were out in force with a particularly strong presence by BBC television who used helicopters to obtain aerial views of the train as it headed north, a method of filming nothing like as common then as now. Even with the two tenders, water was still something of a problem, especially when it was discovered that the water level in the three sets of troughs en route, Scrooby, Wiske Moor and Lucker, had been reduced by BR and not restored to normal for the occasion.

Needless to say, thousands of people lined the route to cheer the train on and it was a truly great event. There were nail-biting moments as there were so many potential obstacles to completing a journey of nearly 400 miles without stopping, even for a second. A broken rail was detected north of Doncaster but by keeping the train moving at walking pace a halt was avoided. Then, at Berwick there was a misunderstanding when the signalman thought the train was going to stop for water when he saw a road tanker standing by, but this was for use in emergency only. The main line signal was set at red and the train was diverted into the goods loop. Again, the train slowed to a crawl in the hope that the signal would go 'off' as it was assumed by the loco crew that there must be an obstruction on the line ahead. When it was realised what was happening, the train continued on through the goods line with the locomotive whistling and the crew shaking their fists at the signalman! Arrival at Edinburgh was made without any further heart-stopping moments and the journey was declared a great success. Another unique landmark had been added to the locomotive's history.

Opposite:
History repeating. Compare these views of 1 May 1968 with that taken 40 years earlier, page 14. No 4472, once again devoid of a headboard, departs from King's Cross on another nonstop run to Edinburgh. *E. M. Rowellan Allan Library*

Left:
As the train got underway on its anniversary run the locomotive found itself working alongside an example of the motive power that had replaced it. 'Deltic' diesel-electric No D9021 *Argyll & Sutherland Highlander* heads the regular 10am 'Flying Scotsman' train — which got there first — by two hours! — at Belle Isle, just outside the London terminus. *Patrick Russell*

TWO TENDERS

Right:
A good study of the two tenders as No 4472 is about to plunge into Gasworks Tunnel with a special from Leeds and Doncaster to King's Cross in connection with the open day at Clapham Transport Museum, 20 October 1968.
Brian Stephenson/ Ian Allan Library

Below:
Even with two tenders no opportunity should ever be missed to replenish the tanks. Wiske Moor troughs are pictured again, this time on 4 May 1968, the occasion of the nonstop return working from Edinburgh to London, King's Cross.
John S. Whiteley

From August 1968 *Flying Scotsman* was the only steam locomotive allowed to run on Britain's main line railways so, on reflection, it is perhaps unfortunate that from September 1969 it was to be away from the UK, with much of the time prior to then being taken up with preparations for its North American tour. The visit to the USA and Canada has been recounted a number of times before so it is thought there is no real need to give a fully detailed itinerary of its American journeys, but a few myths have arisen over the years as to what actually happened, and why this famous British locomotive was nearly lost for all time from its home tracks.

The story actually goes right back to 1965 when the possibilities of a long-term future for operating *Flying Scotsman* on BR appeared to be slim indeed. A suggestion was put to Alan Pegler that year by Mr F. Nelson Blount of Steamtown, Vermont, that the locomotive should visit the USA. The idea was kept very much under wraps while Alan Pegler made some visits to the States where he met railroad officials, government agencies and the Interstate Commerce Commission, to discuss the feasibility and commercial viability of such a venture. Negotiations were proceeding well when tragedy struck — Nelson Blount was killed in a plane crash in 1967. As a result, the project lost not only its instigator but also the funding that was being set up. However, the seeds of the idea had been sown and there were still people and organisations who were keen that the proposal should proceed, if not immediately, then at some time in the future.

The President of the Southern Railway System, W. Graham Claytor Jr, was an enthusiastic and influential supporter. He offered to be official host and negotiated for the exhibition train to run on five other railroads. Flying Scotsman (USA) Ltd was formed to co-ordinate activities, with offices in London and New York.

PREPARATIONS BEGIN

By late 1968 Darlington Works had closed and Doncaster had dispensed with its steam locomotive repair facilities, so for its next overhaul the Pacific went to the Hunslet Engine Co in Leeds where, amongst other work, the boiler was retubed. It was at this time that the North American tour was announced. Before it could be accepted for American operation representatives of the US Transport Commission and Canadian National Railways were flown over to the UK to carry out an inspection which was very thorough. This called for quite a bit of additional dismantling of the locomotive to be undertaken, but they were more than satisfied with what they saw and were happy to grant a North American operating permit.

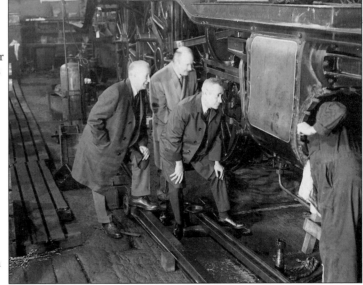

HUNSLET OVERHAUL

The overhaul prior to the North American tour was undertaken by the Hunslet Engine Co Ltd in Leeds. Here, a detailed inspection is made of the stripped-down locomotive by (left to right) William Downie, Railway Mechanic Specialist of the Canadian Transport Commission, Alan Pegler and George W. Johnston, Chief Boiler Inspector of Canadian National Railways. Addressing Mr Johnston through the cylinder is a Hunslet engineer. *Ian Allan Library*

Right:
The boiler and firebox
assembly in Hunslet's
works during the winter
of 1968-9.
Ian Allan Library

Below:
The inside of the boiler
with most of the
tubes removed.
Ian Allan Library

Above:
A general view in Hunslet's works as the
job progresses. *Ian Allan Library*

Left:
The finished article. Immediately prior to
being shipped to North America No 4472
visited BR Doncaster Works for a light
overhaul and the fitting of a few 'extras'.
It is depicted on Friday, 8 August 1969
with cowcatcher, buckeye coupling and
release mechanism, bell and
whistle/hooter. The control wires for
these audible warning devices ran along
the inside of the handrail.
T. Boustead/Ian Allan Library

In addition to the engine and its two tenders, a trade exhibition train of nine coaches was destined for North America. While these vehicles were being prepared there were a few more months in 1969 when No 4472 was able to work further excursions on the British main line. It was as popular as ever wherever it went, the sight of a steam engine on the national rail network now being confined to this locomotive alone.

An unusual working took place in mid-August when four of the exhibition coaches were taken to Liverpool Docks from Twickenham, Middlesex, where they had been converted to their new role. On the last day of the month *Flying Scotsman* headed its final special in the UK, for what turned out to be some considerable time, in fact, for much longer than originally expected.

Before shipment to the USA a few further excursions were run in Britain, the last being on 31 August 1969, an LNER Society special from King's Cross to Newcastle upon Tyne. Photographed between Monkwearmouth and Seaburn, no cowcatcher or buckeye for these workings but the bell and whistle are prominent.
I. S. Carr/Ian Allan Library and G. S Cocks/Ian Allan Library

THE JOURNEY BY SEA

No 4472 is swung high over Brocklebank Branch Dock, Liverpool on the first step of her journey to the USA. In the background, through the morning mist, is the South African SA *Transporter*. *Rodney Wildsmith/ Ian Allan Library*

Right:
Safely on board the *Saxonia* the steel cables are removed as the stevedores prepare to secure the engine for her voyage. *Rodney Wildsmith/ Ian Allan Library*

Above:
Shortly before the *Saxonia* left Liverpool Docks bound for Boston, USA, Alan Pegler ceremonially launched the *Flying Scotsman* export trip by breaking a bottle of champagne over the buffer beam on 19 September 1969. *J. R. Hillier/ Ian Allan Library*

EMIGRATION

The locomotive, two tenders and a further coach, travelled to Liverpool Docks the following month where, on the 19th, they were hoisted aboard the 21,370-ton Cunard turbine steamship *Saxonia* for a 10-day crossing of the Atlantic to Boston, Massachusetts. (The *Saxonia* was later sold by Cunard and upon joining the Soviet Black Sea Shipping Co fleet, was renamed *Leonid Sobinov*.) While on its North Atlantic passage, preparation work continued on the locomotive. A bell and a whistle, as required for operation in the USA, were fitted, these having been donated by Graham Claytor. Also, a buckeye coupling and a cowcatcher, which had been prefabricated at Doncaster, were fitted to the front of the locomotive. Until quite recently at least, the cowcatcher survived, leaning against a wall at Carnforth depot, Lancashire.

Off-loading in Boston Harbor was not straightforward as the dockside cranes were not large enough to reach across the ship and lift the railway equipment, including the two coaches. The way round this was to employ two large US Navy floating cranes to lift the items from the deck of the *Saxonia* and then lower them onto a vintage steam-powered lighter of McKie Lighter Co which could then float close enough to the harbour cranes for transfer to dry land. This manoeuvre was appropriately accompanied by the skirl of Scottish bagpipes. The whole affair attracted much expatriate Scottish interest, thanks to the locomotive's name. Had the locomotive been another member of the class, such as *Firdaussi, Merry Hampton* or *Galopin* for example, the event would probably never have happened. Although this activity was taking place at about 8am on a Sunday, there was great media interest and the US Army permitted railfans and the press into an otherwise restricted area, to view

Above right:
Flying Scotsman is lifted carefully from the deck on arrival at Boston Harbor. Note the spreader beam brought across the Atlantic with the locomotive to aid cranage of this unusal cargo. *Ian Allan Library*

Right:
On shore in the USA Alan Pegler smiles for the cameras as Bob Crabb, the locomotive's resident pipe-major, provides traditional Scottish musical accompaniment. *Ian Allan Library*

the proceedings. The rest of the coaches, all of which were painted in the Pullman colours of chocolate and cream, had arrived earlier, four in August and the other three in mid-September. Although their arrival had not been greeted with such a fanfare of publicity, the first load had proved even more troublesome — and costly — to land. Two of the coaches were found to be out of reach of the cranes on the lighter. The handling of the ship's other cargo had to be stopped and the tugs recalled to tow the ship from its berth, turn it round and re-moor it. This lost the best part of a day in the ship's schedule at a cost of something like $15,000! As the vehicles arrived they were placed in the secure care of Boston army base to protect them from the attention of the youthful vandals of East Boston. Alan Pegler arrived in Boston on the Saturday afternoon before the locomotive's off-loading, having travelled there on the Turbotrain service.

THE AMERICAN TOUR BEGINS

The train was assembled for an unpublicised shake-down trip, on 3 October 1969, from Boston to New London, Connecticut and back, running at about 45mph. This gave the locals their first opportunity to show their 'appreciation' of this magnificent sight, and a rock thrown at the locomotive as it passed left a deep dent in the side which looked as if it had been hit by a bullet. Upon return to Boston the train was placed on public display at South station.

A further modification made for American operation was the fitting of 'dual controls' so that the engine could be driven from either the left or right sides. For this, swivel bars were fitted to the controls, extending across the footplate in front of the firebox.

The official opening ceremony of the travelling exhibition took place at *Flying Scotsman's* traditional time of 10am, on 8 October. Eric Williams, a genuine British butler imported specially for the festivities, climbed up onto the front of the locomotive with a gallon(!) bottle of Cutty Sark Scotch whisky and smashed it against the buckeye coupler. There were groans to be heard from the audience, with both American and British accents... Scots Guard pipe-major Bob Crabb, was on hand with his bagpipes to mark the occasion musically.

Thereafter the tour began in earnest and many famous cities were visited, including New York and Washington, both before the end of the month. Events were arranged whereby No 4472 met up with preserved American steam locomotives, attracting large crowds. The weather had been good right up to the approach to Atlanta, Georgia on 30 October when heavy rain was experienced, but it failed to dampen the enthusiasm of the railfans, many having travelled a considerable distance just to have a sight of this world-famous locomotive.

The only mechanical fault to come to light was caused by the whistle which had been fitted during the sea crossing as it had not been positioned correctly. Consequently, every time it was blown, a shower of dirty water, which had condensed in the long pipe leading from the boiler, was blown back along the side of the cab and the first few coaches. Apart from this fairly minor irritation all was going well, and for the first time the owner was able to take a turn at driving his steed officially. This first tour ended in November 1969 after 39 days and 60,000 people having visited the train. The locomotive and coaches then travelled to Slaton, Texas on the Santa Fe Railroad for winter storage, while a second tour was being organised for the following year. Large, enthusiastic crowds, co-operative railroads and the chance to drive the locomotive at speed through spectacular scenery to many exciting destinations — it all seemed too good to be true...

THERE MAY BE TROUBLE AHEAD...

There was an American law, which presumably needed enforcing only very rarely, stipulating that foreign locomotives visiting the USA could haul only circus or exhibition trains, and that fare-paying passengers could not be conveyed. Knowing this, the train had been promoted as a British trade show with firms invited to support it, and so far, the venture was proving a great success. As recently as the mid-1990s, the prestigious *This England* magazine mentioned the fact that it had a healthy American readership which could be traced back to the promotion it conducted on the *Flying Scotsman* tour of the USA about a quarter of a century earlier. After this good start, the British General Election of June 1970 brought changes in policy. The Board of Trade now considered for example, that an old steam locomotive did not give the right image for British businesses which were now actively discouraged from supporting the venture.

It was not long before the financial input by exhibitors dwindled away, and although many Americans would love to have travelled behind *Flying Scotsman,* this was just not possible under the American law. Alan Pegler was fully aware of the impossible financial situation he was now facing but considered all he could do was press on, regardless, and continue to have a good time while it lasted. The second tour took in the mid USA and Canada, crossing the border on 20 August 1970 by means of the St Clair Tunnel under the river of the same name at Sarnia, Ontario.

The next winter was spent in Canada with No 4472 accommodated in the roundhouse at Spadina, Toronto, but the coaches had to be kept in open storage and were subjected to lengthy periods covered by snow. No snow is the 'right' type for improving rolling stock and it was not long before the paintwork began to peel and roofs showed signs of leaking, with consequent damage to the interiors.

The dream was becoming a nightmare, as every way he turned Alan came up against a problem and mounting costs with ever-declining income. A light at the end of the tunnel appeared to be the chance to participate in British Week in San Francisco and so, in September 1971, No 4472 set off on a 4,500-mile journey with its train in a last ditch attempt to recoup the losses that had by now been incurred. On arrival at the famous west coast port, the locomotive, its two tenders and train were allocated an excellent spot at Fisherman's Wharf. As well as being a scenic location it was a good site for business and the future began to look promising.

The British Week was really only an excuse to get to San Francisco, and it was anticipated that about 18 months of such trading could well put the venture back on its financial course. But *Flying Scotsman* was not alone at this lucrative site and it was not long before other businessmen were pointing out that no less than 92 car parking spaces were being occupied by this train. Therefore, pressure was exerted to have the train moved further down the wharf. This was done, with disastrous financial consquences. Business immediately fell off to practically nothing, and it was all back to square one. By the new year, Alan Pegler could not hold off the creditors any longer and after a friend had bought him an airline ticket, he flew back to London and filed his own petition for bankruptcy. A sad end for a venture that had promised so much in the beginning.

The financially ruined locomotive owner returned to San Francisco to do what he could for the 'old girl' and he was successful in getting her housed safely and securely at the US Army base at Stockton, near Sacramento. He then had to get back to England for the public bankruptcy examination. As he was completely broke the only way he could make the journey was to work for it, so he secured a job as a

ship's entertainer with P&O lines. Alan was a 'natural' and went down very well with the passengers, so much so that he was offered full-time employment at sea. Having now lost everything, there was little choice but to accept a complete change of direction and a new lifestyle. There was now nothing he could do to hold on to *Flying Scotsman,* and what would now happen to the locomotive could not be foretold. Stranded far from home in an American army base, the future looked bleak indeed.

Above right:
No 4472 on display at the Canadian National Exhibition, Toronto on 24 August 1970. Passing on the main line is CNR No 3154, a 1,800hp diesel heading a Windsor-Toronto 'Tempo' service.
C. W. R. Bowman/Ian Allan Library

Right:
Flying Scotsman reverses a train into Montreal Yard, Ballantyne, on 18 September 1970 assisted by CNR Bo-Bo diesel No 8501
C. W. R. Bowman/Ian Allan Library

A night-time view at Spadina Roundhouse, Toronto, 28 August 1970. This was the main motive power depot for Toronto's passenger locomotives where No 4472 received a boiler wash-out. *James A. Brown/Ian Allan Library*

4

A NEW OWNER AND A NEW LEASE OF LIFE

A lan Pegler soon settled into his new career on the high seas, and a couple of years later was able to discharge himself from bankruptcy. His cruising career lasted for nearly seven years with much of his time spent on board P&O Lines' turbo-electric ship *Canberra*. Bitten by the entertaining bug he followed his maritime adventures by taking on the role of 'The King' at the Beefeater Medieval Banquet at the Ivory House in London where he appeared dressed in full Tudor costume and grew bushy side whiskers, which he retains to this day!

Needless to say, the locomotive that had meant so much was not forgotten, nor indeed, was it abandoned. It was a very sensitive issue, and although moves were being made for repatriation of the locomotive, negotiations for its removal from the army base and shipment to the UK had to be carried out with some discretion. There was the slim possibility of a further creditor popping up from somewhere and taking it upon themselves to take possession of the engine as an asset with a view to realising its value, if only as scrap metal. At the time, there was probably only one person able to assist in this matter as this needed to be someone with a sincere interest in the future of the locomotive, and the means with which to provide the cost of transport across the Atlantic.

That person was perhaps as equally well known in British railway preservation circles, Mr 'Bill' McAlpine (now The Hon Sir William McAlpine Bt). As soon as Mr McAlpine had been fully briefed on the situation, wheels began to turn for the rescue. No chances were to be taken so the exercise had to be undertaken as quickly and as quietly as possible. In fact, within little over a week, all known creditors had been paid off and ownership of the engine and two tenders formally passed to him. Transfer of the locomotive from the army base to Oakland Docks took place on 19 January 1973 for loading onto the MV *California Star*. *Flying Scotsman* was lashed to the deck for the long journey by sea, sailing via the Panama Canal and across the North Atlantic, experiencing gales and snow en route, arriving in Liverpool Docks on 13 February 1973.

On board the MV *California Star* prior to being off-loaded by the Mersey Docks & Harbour Co floating crane *Mammoth*, Wednesday, 14 February 1973. The tender is being lifted off the ship. *Thomas C. Bowen/Ian Allan Library*

THE RETURN OF THE 'KING'

Many had resigned themselves by now, to the fact that *Flying Scotsman* was almost certainly lost from the United Kingdom and that steam on the national rail system had, in effect, been confined to history. Only a few years before, it was impossible to imagine the entire network devoid of steam traction, but by the early 1970s, it was virtually unimaginable to visualise steam on such famous routes as the Settle & Carlisle, the North and West or Salisbury to Exeter. Steam-hauled trains would be perpetuated on preserved, single-track branch lines, on average no more than about five miles in length and, invariably, comprising a tank engine hauling two, three or perhaps four coaches.

Although for a while No 4472 was the only steam locomotive permitted to run on BR because of the agreement made at the time of purchase and its subsequent extension, it was of course not available, having been in North America. Other express passenger steam locomotives had been secured from BR prior to scrapping with the intention of developing Alan Pegler's idea of running main line excursions. These had been bought by societies specially created to own and run such locomotives, including *Clan Line*, *Princess Elizabeth* and *Sir Nigel Gresley*, while even fewer, but notable individuals, like David Shepherd, Pat Whitehouse and Mike Higson, had made personal commitments to saving main line motive power. Some could not see a future in keeping such items and correspondence appeared in the railway press condemning the various groups and individuals for endeavouring to procure further locomotives. One correspondent, a well-known member of a mid Wales narrow gauge railway, even suggested that with two LNER 'A4s' preserved in North America and one in the National Collection, any more would be unnecessary duplication. He was of course referring to the project to secure No 4498 *Sir Nigel Gresley*! This blinkered attitude usually has the effect of spurring on even harder those who wish to make a more positive contribution to the railway interest.

However, for the time being, none of these locomotives could venture on to the main line and there appeared to be little hope of a change of policy, but a number of railway activists kept up the pressure for a return of steam specials on the main line. They were able to quote, as example, the earlier and successful operations of *Flying Scotsman*. It was not until October 1971 that the first ray of hope appeared, when ex-GWR 'King' class locomotive No 6000 *King George V* was given the opportunity to tour the country with a train of Pullman cars sponsored by Bulmer's Cider of Hereford. Since then, steam on the main line has grown beyond all recognition, at first over a very limited selection of routes but in recent years few lines have not seen a steam excursion at some time or other and new ground is being broken all the time. Nevertheless, there is always some potential or predicted obstacle-forming legislation looming so that today, more than ever, tour operators have to plan ahead with extreme care and concern for the future. Steam operations should never be taken for granted, whether on the national rail network or on independent railways.

NEW HORIZONS

The repatriation of *Flying Scotsman* in 1973 was greeted with joy and, with an unusual chapter having been added to its history, its reputation and 'pulling power' greatly enhanced. No 4472 was soon in action on BR metals after arrival in the UK, running light from Liverpool to Derby Works where it was checked over and given a light overhaul. The first outward indication that there was a new owner was the fact that the nameplates were given black backgrounds once again, which they have retained ever since.

Safely home and receiving loving attention again at the Paint Shop, BR Derby Works 3 July 1973. *T. Boustead/ Ian Allan Library*

Mr McAlpine formally accepted the locomotive into his care on 14 July, when the then Chairman of the British Railways Board, the Rt Hon Richard Marsh, handed it over at a ceremony at Derby.

But where do you *put* 150 tons of steam locomotive when you have just taken delivery of it? However 'well-heeled' the owner might be, it is still a matter that has to be resolved. After leaving Derby Works the engine worked south to the Torbay Steam Railway (now the Paignton & Dartmouth Steam Railway), making its first extended visit to a preserved railway — something that was to occur frequently in later years. Although a powerful locomotive like this is rather restricted in such situations, including being limited to 25mph running, it does give members of the public an excellent opportunity to get close to the locomotive and inspect it far more easily than when on main line duties. And what a draw for the railway!

The Rt Hon Richard Marsh breaks a bottle of champagne over the buffer beam at the formal acceptance of the locomotive into Mr Bill McAlpine's ownership on 14 July following completion of work at Derby. Mr McAlpine (as he was then) stands behind Mr Marsh while Mr Gray, Derby Works Manager, left, shields his eyes from flying glass and 'bubbly'! *T. Boustead/ Ian Allan Library*

Below:
No 4472 fresh out of Derby Works, 31 July 1973, following acquisition by W. H. McAlpine and repatriation from North America. *Gresley Society Collection*

This was only a temporary solution to the housing problem and at the end of its holiday by the sea the main line beckoned once again. The first special to be worked on BR since the return from the States took place in September when a train was hauled, together with *King George V,* from Newport to Hereford and on to Shrewsbury and back. There were then only a very few private steam railways with main line connections and so a new site with sidings was sought that could give main line access. What appeared to be an ideal location was then acquired by Mr McAlpine and fellow preservationist, The Hon John Gretton, with the intention of establishing a steam centre from where *Flying Scotsman* and the new owner's other locomotive, *Pendennis Castle,* could be operated. (These two engines, which first met up at Wembley in 1925, have had numerous reunions over the years, as related later in the story.) Situated in Rutland, this apparently ideal site was a former iron-stone railway at Market Overton and could so easily have become a major railway centre of national importance.

A group of supporting enthusiasts was established, and as well as looking after this famous duo, they were given the unenviable task of sectionalising the rebuilt 'Merchant Navy' Pacific No 35029 *Ellerman Lines* which had been acquired by the National Railway Museum from the famous locomotive graveyard at Barry in South Wales. Many will be familiar with this exhibit which has had one side cut away to reveal its insides. Much of the work had

Top left:
No 4472 back on BR tracks, 22nd September 1973, double-heading with GWR 4-6-0 No 6000 *King George V* on the outward journey of the 'Atlantic Venturers Express'. They are seen passing Pontypool Road with the Bulmer's Pullman set. *D. E. Canning/Ian Allan Library*

Top right:
Flying Scotsman arrives at its new winter home on 30 October 1973, this being at Market Overton in Rutland, which it was to share with the owner's other engine, No 4079 *Pendennis Castle*. This LNER and GWR pair of locomotives originally met at Wembley in 1925, had the same owner in the 1970s, and then met again many years later on the other side of the world! In this view, however, it is really the *shed* that is of 'historic' interest. This was the first Atcost precast concrete building to be built to metric measurements. It provided condensation-proof and insulated cover for these famous locomotives and accompanying rolling stock. *Atcost Ltd/Ian Allan Library*

Above:
Two of the world's most famous engines and both owned by Mr Bill McAlpine at the time: LNER 'A3' class 4-6-2 No 4472 *Flying Scotsman* and GWR 'Castle' class No 4079 *Pendennis Castle* which today is, regrettably, resident in Australia, although a return to the UK might yet occur. *Rex Coffin/Ian Allan Library*

to be done carefully by hand with hacksaws. When the work was completed it was something all those who had been involved with vowed they would never undertake again! It was almost impossible to move too, so unbalanced was it with most of one side removed.

Unfortunately, however, the main line connection to the site was closed and the track lifted thereby undermining its *raison d'être*. Initially the support group stayed on after the departure of their main line charges and established themselves as the Market Overton Industrial Railway Association, but they too later moved to a new site at Cottesmore where they formed what is today's Rutland Railway Museum.

REGULAR ROUTES AND STARRING ROLES

Following an appearance at Kensington Olympia in early August 1974, No 4472 then moved to its new home at Steamtown, Carnforth with which it was to be associated for many years. This proved to be an ideal base for working main line specials, the majority of which were in the north of England during the 1970s, with No 4472 being one of the most regular and reliable performers. A particularly notable event was attended in August 1975 — the 150th anniversary of the opening of the Stockton & Darlington Railway which was held at Shildon in Co Durham. *Flying Scotsman* appeared together with a large collection of preserved steam locomotives, assembled from all over the country, to mark this historic event, the centenary of which had been celebrated in 1925, when *Flying Scotsman* had been otherwise engaged at Wembley. A grand cavalcade of locomotives through the ages took place on 31 August with No 4472 hauling North Eastern Railway 2-4-0 No 910 from the National Collection and carrying a headboard of sponsors Wm McEwan Brewers.

A memorable special train was worked on 1 May 1976 to mark the centenary of the opening of the Settle & Carlisle line. No 4472 was double headed by the old LNWR 2-4-0 No 790 *Hardwicke* forming a most unusual, and previously unlikely, 'little and large' pairing. Most definitely a combination that had never occurred before and making what could almost be called a comic sight! Such operations are one of the joys of railway preservation.

In November 1977 *Flying Scotsman* was called on once again for film work, but disguised as a different locomotive on each side — long-gone sister 'A3s' No 4474 *Victor Wild* and No 4480 *Enterprise*. The two tenders were used somewhat surprisingly for the sequences which were

When in McAlpine's ownership the second tender was 'disguised' in the blue and light grey BR coaching stock livery of the time and lettered 'Flying Scotsman Enterprises'. It is seen here near Craven Arms on a Central Wales line, Swansea-Shrewsbury, excursion on 6 April 1974.
Paul H. Boot/Ian Allan Library

filmed in the York area. Earlier in the year 'Bill' McAlpine's other main line locomotive, *Pendennis Castle*, had been sold and was exported to Australia. Although it was never to return to the UK, the two old locomotive friends were to meet up again a few years later. Indeed, it was not until then that the truth behind this deal was made known generally. The first choice for the Australian purchase had been none other than *Flying Scotsman*, and although a great deal of persuasion was exerted by the Secretary of the Pilbara Railway Historical Society, they were unsuccessful in their bid. The next best thing they agreed was the nearly as-famous GWR 'Castle' class locomotive.

Above:
No 4472 takes its place in the cavalcade on 31 August 1975 to mark the 150th anniversary of the opening of the Stockton & Darlington Railway. Towed behind is North Eastern Railway 2-4-0 No 910 from the National Collection.
Gavin Morrison

Right:
Today, locomotives are often given false identities for photographers with a perverted view of railway history, but on this occasion, in November 1977, *Flying Scotsman* became two of its long-departed sisters for filming purposes. It is seen at Crossgate, Leeds, en route from Carnforth to York, with this side showing No 4474 *Victor Wild*. The second tender, previously an impressive feature, is in non-matching livery.
Les Nixon

Left:
Up in the air again. From mid-December 1977 until June 1978 an overhaul was carried out at the Barrow-in-Furness engineering works of Vickers Shipbuilding Group Ltd. To gain entry to the boiler shop, No 4472 had to be lifted from one siding to another. The 250-ton crane used was the biggest in the northwest of England. *Vickers Shipbuilding Group Ltd/ Ian Allan Library*

Below left:
Tuesday, 6 June 1978, the engine is propelled at Vickers engineering works, Barrow, by one of its Hudswell, Clarke, 0-4-0 diesel shunters in order to couple the Pacific to its tender following completion of the overhaul. *David Eatwell/Ian Allan Library*

Below:
No 4472 provides the power for a special to commemorate the life of the Rt Rev Eric Treacy, probably one of the most famous railway photographers of all time, who had died at Appleby station in May that year. The 'Lord Bishop' special passes Long Preston, between Hellifield and Settle, on 30 September 1978. *Brian Morrison*

During the late 1970s and early 1980s, steam operation on the main line was confined to specific routes, with trains run on a fairly regular basis, so there was little variety other than an occasional change in motive power. Any new locomotive added to the pool was certainly cause for celebration. *Flying Scotsman* was, of course, a popular and frequently used engine on such trains as the 'Cumbrian Coast Express', 'Cumbrian Mountain Express', the 'North Yorkshireman' and 'Scarborough Spa Express'. Among other trains to be graced by No 4472 was the 'Lord Bishop' on 30 September 1978 which was one of two trains run to commemorate the famous railway photographer, the Rt Rev Eric Treacy who had collapsed and died at Appleby station on the Settle & Carlisle route in May while photographing *Evening Star*, the last steam locomotive built for BR.

Only on very rare occasions has the world's most famous locomotive failed in service, but this did happen in October 1979 while it was returning to Carnforth following a six-day tour which had included an appearance at the now-closed Dinting Railway Centre in Derbyshire. The cause was put down to poor coal, and a Class 25 diesel had to come to the rescue to bank the train on to Carnforth, travelling via Blackburn and Hellifield.

ROCKET 150

Another cavalcade appearance was made in 1980, this time to celebrate 150 years of the Liverpool & Manchester Railway, with a parade of locomotives at Rainhill, culminating in the ill-fated APT (Advanced Passenger Train) and featuring *Flying Scotsman* on all three days, 24-26 March. The locomotives that appeared at 'Rocket 150', as the event was called, were based at the National Coal Board's Bold Colliery and the array of types in their various liveries from many different railways made an impressive and memorable sight, but regrettably, not one accessible to the paying public.

A few days prior to this historic event, *Flying Scotsman* was chosen, although somewhat inappropriately perhaps, to work a philatelic special for the Post Office. This train conveyed covers bearing the Liverpool & Manchester Railway commemorative stamps on the first day of issue,

12 March, from Liverpool Lime Street to Manchester Victoria. This pioneer railway was later to form part of the LNER's rival, the LMS, of course. However, the charisma of the locomotive resulted in few in the Northwest taking exception to this North Eastern interloper. In fact, immediately after Rocket 150, *Flying Scotsman* went on display as the star attraction at the Great Railway Exposition, staged at Manchester Liverpool Road station to mark the 150th anniversary of 'the world's first passenger railway station'. This temporary exhibition was the forerunner of the permanent museum now housed at this historic terminus. It may not necessarily be realised that although the Post Office has issued several sets of stamps commemorating Britain's railways, as yet, none has depicted *Flying Scotsman*. The 17p stamp in a set of five issued in 1985 was titled 'The Flying Scotsman', but this was an illustration of an 'A4' streamlined Pacific heading the *train* of that name and ever since has caused a degree of confusion among those not so well informed.

TENDER WORK

The next couple of years saw many main line outings, but the locomotive had to be withdrawn from service on 30 July 1982 as its tender was leaking badly. For some time there had been a trickle of water from the back of the tender, but the corrosion became too bad and a new tender tank was required. The tender was stripped down at Carnforth and the chassis overhauled while a new tank was fabricated by the Wakefield Skillcentre, as the quotes from private contractors were considered too high. The college had some reservations about tackling such a job, so a quarter-size model was built first, but the 12 trainees produced a fine piece of work which was regarded as indistinguishable from the Doncaster-built original.

You cannot keep a good locomotive down and so while this work was in progress *Flying Scotsman* borrowed the tender from 'A4' Pacific No 4498 *Sir Nigel Gresley* which was to undergo its seven-year boiler examination during the winter of 1982/3. This tender was repainted from garter blue livery into apple green but retained its cast, silver LNER lettering and was attached to the 'A3' until 1984.

By 1983 a number of other steam locomotives were becoming available for main line operations and there were murmurings among some enthusiasts that *Flying Scotsman* was receiving just a bit too much attention. If that was the case then these critics were in for a disappointing year as this was the locomotive's Diamond Jubilee and it was certainly not going to be overshadowed by any former scrapyard occupants! A small exhibition was staged at Steamtown Carnforth to mark the occasion but it was three notable main line runs that really stamped the locomotive's authority on the preservation scene.

Above:
With suitable adornments to mark the locomotive's Diamond Jubilee, 1923-83, No 4472 is pictured in immaculate condition at Doncaster Works on 26 February 1983. Several specials were run to mark this occasion but only as far south as Peterborough on the ECML due to elecrification work. At this time, the tender was undergoing attention and so the usually blue-liveried tender was borrowed from A4 Pacific No 4498 *Sir Nigel Gresley*, this being distinguishable here by the raised cast-metal LNER lettering. *Peter Harris/Ian Allan Library*

Opposite:
The ex-LNER Pacific at Tuebrook sidings, Liverpool, after having worked the Liverpool & Manchester Railway 150th anniversary special from Manchester on 12 March 1980. Surprisingly, perhaps, in view of the occasion, it was used in preference to an LMS locomotive. *David Dyson*

ECML, OVER THE BORDER, AND A ROYAL OCCASION

On 27 February No 4472 returned to its old stamping ground, the East Coast main line no less, working a special from Peterborough to York, and making the return journey on 6 March. Huge crowds turned out to witness these trains, so obviously not everyone thought the 'old girl' was 'overexposed', but the down side was the dreadful examples of trespass with people putting themselves in danger on the lineside to get a better view. These anniversary workings were probably among the most memorable run by the locomotive in the UK during its ownership by W. H. McAlpine. The 80th anniversary celebrations are awaited with interest — they are not *that* far away now!

Later in the year, the 'A3' made one of its rare appearances in Scotland when it attended the Ayr depot open weekend at the end of October in the company of 'A4' No 60009 *Union of South Africa* and No 46229 *Duchess of Hamilton* among others, but it was the following month when it was to make history again.

On Saturday, 10 November 1984 No 4472 headed the Steam Locomotive Operators Association (SLOA) Pullman train, the 'Fenman', from Manchester Victoria to Spalding in Lincolnshire but the return working by this engine was not due to take place until 24 November. No other appearances in the meantime had been announced so it appeared that it was to have a two-week rest in the Fens. But this was not quite the case and SLOA and Steamtown Carnforth personnel had been sworn to secrecy for security reasons as to the real reason for its visit to East Anglia. *Flying Scotsman* had been chosen to work a Royal train conveying HRH The Queen Mother and as such, would be the first preserved steam locomotive to haul an official royal train. The occasion was the formal opening of the North Woolwich Old Station Museum on Tuesday, 20 November.

The previous Saturday the Pacific travelled light engine from March depot to Stratford (London), the last part of the journey, under the wires, with a Class 31 diesel locomotive attached. For such an important train a trial run was made on the Monday which was just as well as it was discovered that there was less than an inch clearance under some of the bridges. A slow and careful passage was called for at these locations, but it was otherwise deemed OK once the old smoke ducts had been removed from a footbridge on the approach to Woolwich station.

The big day came which was bright and sunny and the locomotive was given a white-painted cab roof which was something of a trademark for Stratford depot's diesel locomotives. The driver for this event, including the run from March and the rehearsal, was Tony Gooding, a railwayman of 36 years standing, who was later to declare this the most memorable three days of his career. Her Majesty boarded the train at Stratford Low Level station for the short journey to North Woolwich, travelling in Pullman Parlour Car No 351, which coincidentally, is today, part of Flying Scotsman Railways' Pullman fleet. The train arrived dead on time at North Woolwich where the crew were presented to the Queen Mother. Fireman Reggie Rowe then presented her with a framed painting of *Flying Scotsman* by Arthur Gills, a goods guard based at Temple Mills.

Then, HM The Queen Mother, at the age of 84, was invited to step onto the footplate of the locomotive, which she gladly accepted. She stood for several minutes, chatting to the crew and looking at the fire and cab controls before stepping down onto the platform and making her way to the museum which is located in the station building, just across the platform. The train was then pulled out of the station by a Class 47 diesel to Custom House where the 'A3' was uncoupled from the rear of the train and ran light to Stratford depot having completed its royal duty. Although conveying a member of the royal family the train had been given the reporting number 1G01 rather than the traditional code for royal trains, 1X01, and so the locomotive had not been able to carry the four white headlamps associated with such workings. Those involved were somewhat disappointed as this would have been a unique occurrence.

The timing of the museum opening special was critical as *Flying Scotsman* was due for its seven-year boiler examination which was to keep it out of action for the whole of the following year, so it could easily have missed such a prestigious occasion. The locomotive returned to its base at Carnforth where stripping down in readiness for its boiler lift was started on New Year's Day 1985. When completion of this work was imminent at the end of the year, one magazine included a prophetic reference to the 'A3' in its 'light-hearted glance forward to 1986' where many humorous, but on the whole, unlikely predictions were made. For January it was suggested that *Flying Scotsman* was to be 'repainted as BR No 60103 with double chimney and German-type smoke deflectors, but for Easter only...' How we all laughed!

CAPITAL TRAINS AND ETHEL

As LNER No 4472, the locomotive worked down to London on 27 December, its overhaul now complete, to be based for a while at Marylebone, from where a number of steam specials were being run on a regular basis to Stratford-upon-Avon. Its arrival in the capital was greeted by a Scottish piper — what other locomotive gets such a welcome? The depot name was painted on the buffer beam in small letters, in true LNER style. In addition to heading the 'Shakespeare Limited', a private charter was run on Sunday 12 January, also to Stratford-upon-Avon. This was the 'Half-Century Limited' to mark the owner's birthday! Not all was plain sailing however as a regulator valve problem resulted in the engine being replaced on another private working scheduled for 26 January. This was to convey the Royal Shakespeare Company from London to Stratford-upon-Avon. Further mechanical problems arose in May with various remedial work carried out on the locomotive at its Marylebone base, thereby extending its stay in the Capital.

An unusual, and far from popular feature of steam-hauled trains at this time was the use of what was described as a 'mobile

Top:
On 27 February 1988 *Flying Scotsman* made the long journey from Carnforth to Ruislip. It was photographed passing through Rotherham Masborough station with one of the dreaded ETHEL train-heating diesel units behind the tender. *Hugh Ballantyne*

Above:
No 4472 on the former LSWR main line at Templecombe station, Somerset, while working one of the series of 'Blackmoor Vale Express' trains from Salisbury to Yeovil Junction and back, on 13 June 1987. *Author*

electric train heating locomotive', or ETHEL for short. This was a converted Class 25 Bo-Bo diesel electric locomotive (a type nicknamed 'Rats' by enthusiasts at the best of times) which was coupled between the steam locomotive and the passenger stock to provide electric train heating (ETH). The reason quoted was that the Mark 1 coaching stock then in operation was suffering from corrosion of the steam heating pipes so that equipment could not be used. The first time this 'device' saw service on the 'Shakespeare Limited' of 28 December, the diesel engine actually cut out at High Wycombe. Not only did this make it unable to provide train heat but it lost its air braking and so, to the relief of all, it had to be removed from the train and shunted ignominiously into a siding. *Flying Scotsman* then continued on to Stratford-upon-Avon, unaided and supplying perfectly satisfactory steam heating for its train. However, this was only a temporary reprieve for photographers, who did not like the look of a diesel behind the steam locomotive, and sound recorders who objected to the uncharacteristic noise of a steam-hauled train sounding like a diesel! No doubt somewhere, there was a vintage diesel enthusiast complaining about the steam locomotive obscuring his view... For a few seasons the ETHELS were seen, and heard, behind a number of express engines going about their duties.

A remarkable occurrence took place on 11 October when the Gresley Pacific was joined in London by two streamlined 'A4s', Nos 4498 *Sir Nigel Gresley* and 4468 *Mallard*. The latter, the world speed record holder, had been restored to full working order and released from the National Railway Museum at

York for a series of rail tours. All three Pacifics were lined up to produce a unique spectacle when they were posed together outside the depot at Marylebone; a sight to gladden the heart of any fan of Gresley's locomotive masterpieces.

No 4472 was to have one of its busiest ever years in preservation in 1987, working a large number of trains including private charters. From Friday, 29 May it was to see action on no less than 10 consecutive days, which must be a unique achievement for any preserved steam locomotive on the main line. Duties were far ranging and varied too, starting with film work at Carnforth, followed the next day by the 'Nuclear Coast Express', as this particular train was dubbed, then to Coalville depot, Leicestershire for an open day. For the next five days the 'Cromwell Pullman' was operated on behalf of a tool company, running between Tyseley, Birmingham and Leicester and finally, the 'Blackmoor Vale Express', from Salisbury to Yeovil Junction on Saturday, 6 June and the 'Sunday Luncheon Express', from Salisbury the day after. Phew!

CARNFORTH WORKINGS

The aforementioned 'nuclear' train was the first of several operated on behalf of British Nuclear Fuels Ltd (BNFL) to their Sellafield Reprocessing Plant in Cumbria. The nuclear fuel industry had a particularly poor image at the time and was desperate to prove that it was not all bad and that their power stations were perfectly safe places to visit. The idea was hatched to run a series of five special trains from London to the Sellafield Nuclear Exhibition Centre so that people could see for themselves how safe it all was. It was all rather a clever marketing ploy really as Flying ScotsmanEnterprises Pullman Rail had been experiencing a drop off in patronage of their 'Cumbrian Coast Expresses' which terminated at Sellafield as there were persistent rumours of radioactive leaks from the nearby power station. Now, the place itself was to be the attraction and the operating costs underwritten by BNFL. It was realised that there could be no greater draw than the most famous steam locomotive in the world, which was to work the trains from Carnforth, along the Cumbrian coast to Sellafield.

The trains were officially named the 'Sellafield Sightseers', the first being scheduled for Saturday, 25 April with an encouraging number of advance bookings and enquiries being made. Come the day, and the train was filled with passengers who enjoyed the bonus of a return working from Sellafield behind Bulleid 'West Country' class No 34092 *City of Wells* since there was insufficient time for the 'A3' to be turned upon arrival as it would have had to run on to Eskmeals Gun Range. However, it was not the motive power that attracted the attention of the media on this occasion. Almost inevitably, anti-nuclear protestors seized the opportunity for some publicity with two of them handcuffing themselves to *Flying Scotsman's* boiler handrail when a photographic stop was made at Grange-over-Sands. Departure was held up as they had to be released by British Transport Police. The return train was delayed further by a hoax bomb warning, but arrival in London was only about an hour down on schedule.

Further trains were run without incident and later ones had No 4472 working out and back from Carnforth as it was able to turn on the triangle of track within the power station. This had been suitably upgraded to take this locomotive which is somewhat larger and heavier than the plant's own diesel shunting engines.

Among the many specials worked in 1987, was the 'South Yorkshireman' for Hertfordshire Railtours which set a distance record for preserved steam traction on the main line of 379 miles 39 chains in one day. A couple of other notable trains were run in October — the 'Morecambe Bay Express' on the 17th and the 'Midland Scotsman' on the 25th — both organised by Hertfordshire Railtours to mark the 40th anniversary of the formation of British Railways. The actual date of vesting day for Nationalisation was, of course, 1 January 1948, but late autumn is a much better time to run such trains than the depths of winter, especially so as 'No ETHELS' was given as a guarantee in the advertising.

Before the winter was through, *Flying Scotsman* was moved down from Carnforth to a new home in London which has been its base ever since, even though it has not always been in residence. This is a building that was part of the old GWR locomotive depot at Southall where this much travelled engine was to be prepared, ready for its next great adventure, its most ambitious yet.

4472

IN LIVING COLOUR

Top:
No 60103 *Flying Scotsman* in BR days with double chimney and no smoke deflectors — the form in which it appears today. Photographed in August 1960 heading the down 'Yorkshire Pullman' at Hadley Wood. *J. F. Aylard/ Colour-Rail*

Above:
With German-style smoke deflectors fitted, No 60103 roars through Hitchin on an up express in 1962. *R. Hill/Colour-Rail*

In superb external condition, No 60103 approaches Grantham on a down express in June 1962. *P. J. Hughes/Colour-Rail*

Above:
One of *Flying Scotsman's* many historic occasions. The 'old girl' awaits departure from King's Cross with the highly publicised last run in British Railways' ownership, 14 January 1963. *R. Hill/Colour-Rail*

Right:
Making one of its first public appearances after preservation, No 4472 is seen at Quainton Road station on 18 June 1963 with the Railway Preservation Society's 'Great Central Special'. *R. C. Riley*

Right:
No 4472 makes a superb sight on Western Region metals at Sapperton Bank, Gloucestershire on 16 August 1964. *R. C. Riley*

Below:
In immaculate condition, No 4472 poses at York having worked the 'White Rose' special on 1 May 1966. Distinguishing features at this time were the red-backed nameplates and the green cylinder covers, a 'trademark' of Darlington Works where it had previously received attention. *Colour-Rail*

Top:
The 'Scarborough Flyer' leaves York on the return from Scarborough, 6 April 1968, the locomotive now having the benefit of two tenders. *Les Nixon*

Above:
With two tenders in use again on 12 May 1968, this time on the 'Norfolk Enterprise' special from King's Cross to Norwich. *Colour-Rail*

Top:
The Gresley Pacific returns to York from the Stockton & Darlington Railway 150th anniversary celebrations at Shildon, together with GWR 'Modified Hall' class 4-6-0 No 6960 *Raveningham Hall* and an assortment of rolling stock on 2 September 1975 — 200 miles from Edinburgh.
Les Nixon

Above:
A strange but memorable pairing as the 'A3' double-heads with LNWR No 790 *Hardwicke* at Kents Bank en route to Ravenglass, Cumbria 8 May 1976. The 2-4-0 had been a very successful 'racer' in its time so no doubt it set the pace for the day! *Les Nixon*

Above right:
A stunning and unrepeatable view as No 4472, with two tenders, is seen at Shap summit (19.30) with the 'North Eastern' rail tour of 29 June 1969. This line has of course since been 'marred' with overhead wire equipment.
Les Nixon

Left:
Fitted with cowcatcher and headlamp, No 4472 races through green fields in Canada during its extended tour of North America in 1970.
Robin Russell/ Ian Allan Library

Above:
Flying Scotsman heads through Shipley on a glorious summer's day with a Carnforth-York working on 26 June 1977. *Les Nixon*

Right
No 4472 has travelled between Settle & Carlisle on many occasions since being acquired for preservation and is sure to see action on this route again before too long under its present ownership. Seen here passing Settle Junction signalbox on 26 April 1980. *Colour-Rail*

Right:
Secured to the deck of the aptly named container ship, *New Zealand Pacific*, No 4472 is waiting to set sail from Tilbury Docks on the evening of Sunday, 11 September 1988 bound for the other side of the world.
Nick Pigott

Above:
On 14 August 1989 *Flying Scotsman* became the first steam locomotive to arrive at Alice Springs via the standard gauge line which had been completed in 1980, replacing the notoriously poor condition 3ft 6in gauge tracks. *Nick Pigott*

Above right:
On tour in Australia, *Flying Scotsman* storms past North Goulburn en route to Moss Vale, 21 May 1989. *Martin Bennett*

Right:
No 4472 double-heads No 3801, a New South Wales Government Railways 'C38' class Pacific, and takes water at Goulburn after arrival from Sydney on 24 June 1989. *Martin Bennett*

Above:
Home at last.
Safely back
from its
Australian tour,
the 'A3', still
appearing in
pristine
condition, is
lowered onto
the quayside at
Tilbury Docks
on 14 December
1989 by the
floating crane
London Samson.
Brian Morrison

No 4472 has visited many of Britain's steam railways and is seen here
leaving Bridgnorth on the Severn Valley Railway with the 14.50 to
Kidderminster on 13 October 1991, the last day of its stay.
Hugh Ballantyne

Right:
Back on the main line and working 'under the wires' at Cambridge on 20 October 1991, *Flying Scotsman* approaches the station with the 11.35 'WA&GN Express' from King's Lynn.
Brian Morrison

Right:
Nearing the end of its main line career for some considerable time, No 4472 passes Ais Gill with a southbound 'Cumbrian Mountain Express' on 12 September 1992.
Hugh Ballantyne

Below:
By now confined to private railways, No 4472 found the next best thing to the main line on the Great Central Railway. Here it heads the 15.00 Loughborough to Leicester North at Woodthorpe on 13 December 1992.
Hugh Ballantyne

Left:
In BR guise as No 60103, *Flying Scotsman* pauses at Goodrington Sands on the Paignton & Dartmouth Steam Railway, 18 August 1993. The 'world's most famous locomotive' just manages to provide a quick distraction from the daily newspaper. *Author*

Left:
BR livery and number, smokebox door number plate, double chimney and German-style smoke deflectors made the engine look so different from Alan Pegler's apple green machine that many Dorset and Devon residents could not accept this was the *real Flying Scotsman* when it visited the Swanage and Paignton & Dartmouth railways at this time. Running-round at Kingswear, P&DR, August 1993. *Author*

Returning to the Severn Valley Railway, now in BR livery, the Pacific heads across Victoria Bridge on 23 October 1994 with the 14.45 Bridgnorth-Kidderminster. *Hugh Ballantyne*

Above:
In the delightful setting of Llangollen station on the Llangollen Railway — a railway at which fate seems to have played its hand in the locomotive's fortune — No 60103 is readied for the 'Mid-day Belle' dining train on 5 March 1995. *Author*

Below:
Driver training in progress. *Flying Scotsman* at Llangollen on 6 March 1995. *Author*

Above and right:
In limbo. During late 1995 all major work stopped on the restoration then underway at Southall and rumours abounded regarding the locomotive's future. This is how the locomotive was found on a visit in September. *Author*

Above:
The newly restored No 4472 *Flying Scotsman* is seen on display at the National Railway Museum, July 1999.
Chris Dixon

Left:
The third passenger working following its three-year, £750,000 overhaul, was the 'Sarum Scotsman', the destination on 25 July 1999 being Salisbury.
Author

5

THE GREAT AUSTRALIAN ADVENTURE

By the late 1980s No 4472 *Flying Scotsman* had become, without question, the 'most famous locomotive in the world' — and it did not now need a PR company to say so. If anybody was stopped in the street and asked to name a couple of locomotives they would reply immediately, '*Flying Scotsman*, and, er, Stephenson's *Rocket*...' or perhaps, '*Royal Scot*'. But the first would be without hesitation, and they would almost certainly claim to have seen it at some time in the past, and possibly even to 'have been *on* it'. Another locomotive, also a Gresley-designed Pacific, but one of his streamlined 'A4s', also has rather a strong claim to fame. This is No 4468 *Mallard*, which, to this day, is the holder of the world speed record for steam traction. This mechanical masterpiece attained a speed of 126mph, or the less memorable 202.8km/h, on one notable and well-documented run on 3 July 1938 which was never to be approached, let alone beaten, by any other steam locomotive anywhere else in the world.

This locomotive is, perhaps not surprisingly, part of the National Collection and is normally displayed as a static exhibit at York. However, it was restored to full main line working order for a series of glorious special runs in 1987/8 to mark the 50th anniversary of its record. This work had been undertaken at the instigation of the Friends of the National Railway Museum and had been one of their founding objectives. Meanwhile, on the other side of the world, a number of enthusiasts had also developed a strong interest in *Mallard* and had started to hatch a scheme to get this very notable engine to visit Australia for an event they were organising, Aus Steam '88. This was to be a very important occasion forming part of the country's bicentennial celebrations. The National Railway Museum received no less than four separate requests from organisations in Australia stating that transport would be arranged courtesy of P&O Lines and pointing out that the costs paid would go a long way towards financing the locomotive's next boiler overhaul. Although these proposals were considered for

a while, it was accepted in the end that *Mallard* was just too important an exhibit in the UK, especially during its anniversary year to let go, even for a limited period. Therefore, much to the relief of British enthusiasts, the offer was declined.

Then, in a surprise move in early 1988, it was announced that *Flying Scotsman* was to be shipped to Australia not only to participate in the event but to make an extensive tour of the country. Before negotiations went too

On Saturday, 17/Sunday, 18 December 1988 No 4472 returned to Sydney with a tour train of water gin, five ACT Division cars and a van. Late on the Saturday afternoon the train crosses Wagga Wagga Viaduct, New South Wales. *R. Coles, courtesy Hugh Ballantyne*

far, assurances were obtained regarding the return of the locomotive to Great Britain to ensure there was no repetition of past experiences, but for once in its life, *Flying Scotsman* had not been the first choice!

The initial plan was for the locomotive to be away from the UK for six to eight months only, including shipping time, but the stay in Australia was later extended so that it was eventually absent from the British main line for more than a year, from September 1988 until December 1989. Prior to departure, a thorough overhaul took place at Southall, the work including the fitting of an air pump between the frames so that it could haul the air-braked coaching stock used in Australia. In August, the locomotive was given a test run when it worked a Sunday luncheon train to Stratford-upon-Avon and back even though it was devoid of lining and lettering.

This was to be its only outing between overhaul and shipment and when it travelled to Tilbury Docks it was behind a Class 37 diesel locomotive, No 37358, carrying the appropriate name, *P & O Containers*. Well, No 4472 was sailing P&O Lines, but not in a container of course! On 11 September the locomotive was craned on board the container ship *New Zealand Pacific* and secured as deck cargo. The following day the ship set sail on a five-week voyage to Sydney, via the Cape of Good Hope, arriving on 16 October.

The 28,000-mile tour of Australia was an epic and historic undertaking, visiting the capital cities of all six mainland states: Brisbane in Queensland, Sydney in New South Wales, Melbourne in Victoria, Adelaide in South Australia, Alice Springs in Northern Territory and Perth in Western Australia. A remarkable achievement, ensuring that no other locomotive could come anywhere near its claim of being the world's most famous locomotive. The Australian adventure would be a book in itself and a video or two, but here, only the more notable occasions of this incredible tour can be mentioned.

Soon after arrival at Sydney, *Flying Scotsman* travelled down to Melbourne for participation in Aus Steam '88, the prime objective of the round-the-world trip. It was greeted with wild enthusiasm there, and everywhere it went it drew huge crowds, in the region of 130,000 attending the main event. As many trains as possible were to be worked, with 32 planned but many more were added to the schedule. All were complete sell outs, and some were not cheap either.

While in the state of Victoria, the speed record for steam traction in Australia was broken, even if it could not be claimed officially at the time. This stood at 79mph, held by a Victorian Railways' 'S' class Pacific since the 1930s. On a run from Benella to Seymour *Flying Scotsman* clocked up a speed of nearly 84mph, but the line had a speed restriction of 50mph.

Whenever possible, *Flying Scotsman* met up with local preserved locomotives, sometimes running on parallel tracks, with some unusual combinations of motive power as Australia has main lines of three different track gauges. In addition to standard (4ft 8^1/$_2$in) there are 3ft 6in and 5ft 3in gauges, but a

A rare and spectacular sight as *Flying Scotsman* runs line abreast with Victorian Railways 'R' class Hudson (4-6-4) locomotives Nos R761 and R707 at Dysart, two miles from Seymour, Victoria, on Sunday, 6 August 1989. *Graham Withers/ Ian Allan Library*

regauging programme to spread the standard gauge was sufficiently advanced to enable this extensive tour to be made, right across southern Australia without interruption. This was not the only locomotive to travel to the six capitals during the bicentennial celebrations however, as Australia's most famous locomotive, No 3801, undertook a similar but less eventful itinerary. This handsome locomotive is also painted in apple green and is a 4-6-2 but otherwise is very different in appearance. It is a 'bullet-nosed', semi-streamlined engine of the New South Wales Government Railway 'C38' class which was in service from 1943 until 1965. The first time these two Pacifics were seen together was at Aus Steam '88 and as well as running on parallel tracks they also double-headed a 12-day excursion from Sydney to Brisbane.

In August 1989 the Gresley Pacific set off from Melbourne, destined for Alice Springs. This was a 26-day tour with tickets costing about £1,000 but all were sold well in advance. En route at Seymour the rare and spectacular sight of three abreast running was possible with two other steam locomotives. On Tuesday the 8th, the section from Parkes to Broken Hill produced yet another record for No 4472 — the longest ever nonstop run for a steam locomotive. It ran a total distance of no less than 422 miles 7.59 chains in 9¹/₂hr without stopping. In all, no less than seven drivers were on the regulator in turn. To avoid having to stop for safe-working purposes, the line being worked by staff and ticket, a railwayman was positioned at each passing loop to exchange the staff-ticket as the train passed by. These tickets were carried in cane hoops.

The train left Parkes at 05.00 in order to be ahead of three freight trains that leave there every Tuesday morning, and it arrived at Broken Hill at 14.20, the average speed being approximately 50mph. Four trains were crossed en route, while 16,000gal of water and 10 tonnes of coal were consumed. The record attempt was nearly thwarted on a couple of occasions; the first was when a truck dashed across in front of the train on a level crossing and a collision was only narrowly avoided, by luck rather than judgement. On the second occasion the loco driver failed to catch the staff at one of the crossing loops but even this eventuality had been considered beforehand and a person riding in a service van was able to catch up with the train and make the handover! This was all rather different to what could be done back home on the railways of Britain; five-mile branch lines with 25mph speed restrictions would seem somewhat tame after this!

Sunday, 13 August saw No 4472 working from Tarcoola to Alice Springs, a distance of 490 miles and something which would have been quite impossible a few years earlier. The line had always been 3ft 6in gauge until the conversion to standard gauge throughout, from Adelaide (966 miles) was completed in 1981. This was the route of the famous 'Ghan', for many years a decrepit train picking its way along ageing trackwork and purported to be the world's slowest train. Today, the service is operated with modern, luxury diesel-hauled expresses. The

No 4472 races up the long bank to Glenrowan where the infamous bushranger Ned Kelly and his gang tried to hold up a train in 1880. Three members of the gang were killed and Kelly was captured wearing his home-made armour. He was later hanged. The sun is setting on the first day of the incredible journey from Melbourne to Alice Springs on Sunday, 6 August 1989.
Graham Withers/ Ian Allan Library

British visitor was in fact the first-ever steam locomotive to traverse the new line and it also hauled its heaviest load ever — 735 tons gross — as far as Roe Creek, about 10 miles short of Alice Springs. The train consisted of 15 vehicles including two water bowsers which were often used while in Australia to replenish the tender, a 70-ton coal wagon — and a General Motors Co-Co diesel locomotive. The diesel was hauled dead (no ETHEL this) but was included in the train 'just in case' of emergencies. In the unlikely event of the steam locomotive failing the train would have become stranded in the middle of the desert, which was something best avoided. Of course, it didn't and the diesel locomotive turned out to be more of a burden than a help but those on board the train were no doubt comforted by the thought.

In many ways the visit to Alice Springs was the crowning achievement of the whole Australian adventure. It is one of the most remote railway stations on Earth and it was this journey that a number of the people who were directly connected with *Flying Scotsman* decided to sample. The then owner, The Hon W. H. McAlpine and his wife Jill, flew out from the UK specially to join the train, as did Flying Scotsman Services Chief Executive, Bernard Staite, as well as former Steamtown Carnforth Managing Director, George Hinchcliffe. They met up with the Chief Engineer of the locomotive, Roland Kennington, who accompanied the locomotive from England and during the whole time it was away from these shores and who features prominently later in the story. Also present were support driver

Dave Rollins and 71-year-old mechanic, Fred Steinle, making it a very British occasion. The arrival at Alice Springs was a remarkable spectacle as huge crowds gathered at the station and its approaches to welcome the train. This is a very sparsely populated part of the continent so, to make up such a large number of people, many must have travelled hundreds of miles to be present at this unforgettable occasion.

The next highlight of the tour was one of the most incredible locomotive reunions ever to have taken place when, on 17 September 1989, *Flying Scotsman* met up once again with expatriate No 4079

Above right:
A proud owner, Bill McAlpine, receives a 'pop star' welcome as he is mobbed by well-wishers after the arrival of the locomotive at what is almost certainly the world's most remote station. *Nick Pigott*

Right:
Perhaps the *real* 'Mr Flying Scotsman' is Roland Kennington, the locomotive's chief engineer, seen in the fireman's seat prior to departure from Goulburn, Australia, heading for Sydney on 24 June 1989. *Martin Bennett*

Pendennis Castle. Remember how they had first been seen together as arch rivals at the British Empire Exhibition in 1925? And how they had met up again on several subsequent occasions until parting company in Leicestershire when the 'Castle' was sold to Australia in preference to the Gresley Pacific? Early on in negotiations for the antipodean venture it was suggested that it would be a fantastic opportunity to get these two friendly rivals back together again, but the costs involved in transporting them to a mutually convenient, or rather the least inconvenient location, appeared to put it out of the question as Australia is such a vast landmass.

Such was the success of the tour however that the stay was extended twice so that eventually it was possible to include a really epic journey across the Nullarbor Plain to Kalgoorlie and Perth in Western Australia. Thus, another 'first' for the 'A3' as no other steam locomotive had travelled the whole width of the continent under its own power. This journey included the longest section of dead straight track anywhere in the world — 299 miles. Perth businessman, Ian Willis, whose engineering company has built a number of miniature steam locomotives, put up the six-figure sum required for this operation as it was a personal ambition to see the two British locomotives together. This was a real bonus added on to the end of the tour, even if it would mean that the engine could not be back in the UK until December. The result of this however, would be having to miss out on the opportunity of working Santa specials on the Nene Valley Railway at Peterborough...

A ceremonial 'kissing' of buffers was arranged to take place at Perth where *Pendennis Castle* had arrived on 4 September. This famous Great Western engine had been transported by road the 1,000 miles from its home on the Hammersley Iron Railway, which it had not previously left since delivery there in 1974. A Highland pipe band heralded the arrival of *Flying Scotsman* on the 17th, 9min late, but it had just completed a 2,000-mile rail journey. However, when it came to moving the two locomotives together to touch, the manoeuvre had to be abandoned at the last minute and the two had to face each other at a distance. The reason for this was purely and simply the fact that the huge crowd that had turned out to witness the event was spilling all over the tracks, in and around the engines, making any further movement impossible!

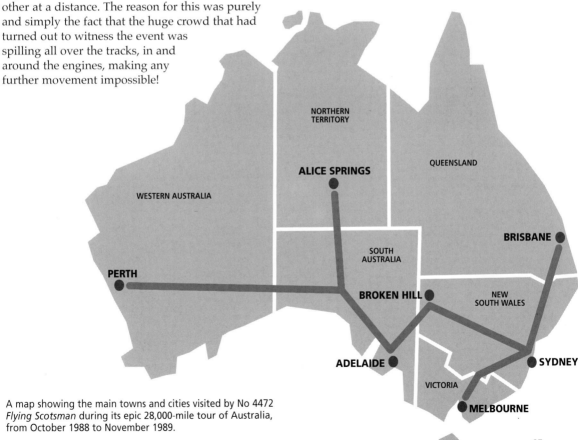

A map showing the main towns and cities visited by No 4472 *Flying Scotsman* during its epic 28,000-mile tour of Australia, from October 1988 to November 1989.

On 24 September, the two record breakers did come together, buffer to buffer, when they worked a special over the Darling Range mountains to Northam. There, they made yet another spectacular and unforgettable sight for all those who were lucky enough to be present when they ran side by side on parallel tracks. A further double-headed train was worked on 8 October before the LNER 4-6-2 had to start heading the long way back to Sydney on the first stage of its homeward journey to Great Britain.

This was not the only reunion that Flying Scotsman made while in Australia, though. A reader's letter in *Steam Railway* magazine told the story of an old King's Cross driver, John Dodds, who had emigrated to Australia many years before, and was pottering in his garden when he suddenly heard the unmistakable sound of a three-cylinder Gresley Pacific coming across the valley. He immediately jumped in his car and drove as fast as he could to Waterfall which was a watering stop and where he caught up with the engine. He was invited on to the footplate where he reacquainted himself with a once-familiar workplace and snatched a quick conversation with the crew, one of whom was also an old King's Cross man. It can be imagined that as he got down from the cab and watched the locomotive steaming into the distance he must have wondered if he had really been dreaming!

The last run in Australia was an out and back working from Darling Harbour in Sydney to Gosford, a short hop of 56 miles. It was now November 1989 and the return to England could not be put off any longer. The locomotive was hauled, dead, to Sydney Harbour where *Titan*, the massive floating crane of Cockatoo Dockyard was waiting to lift the engine, followed by the tender, onto the deck of the French container ship, *La Perouse*. The voyage home via Cape Horn took 40 days, arriving at Tilbury Docks on Wednesday, 14 December. The media was out in force, ready to welcome and record the arrival of the most famous and now, the undisputed most-travelled locomotive in the world, and the first to have circumnavigated the globe. No 4472 was arriving from its triumphant and highly successful tour of Australia where it had run more than 28,000 miles, in far grander style than its previous low-key return from the USA, 17 years before.

No time was to be wasted in getting the 'old girl' back onto British tracks, so it was straight to Southall, where Roland Kennington, also freshly back from Australia, immediately set to on an overhaul, including the removal of the air brake equipment. It was back to the familiar routine, for the time being anyway.

A more triumphant return to the UK than the previous time, No 4472 is off-loaded at Tilbury Docks by floating crane *London Samson*, on 14 December 1989. *Brian Morrison*

4472

Whathad been first hinted at in jest was now becoming more of a possibility. On completion of its post Australian overhaul at Southall, *Flying Scotsman* was being talked about as reappearing in a new, or rather an earlier, guise. This would be with a double chimney once again and accompanying German-style smoke deflectors, and finished in BR Brunswick green with the number 60103. However, there was pressure from other quarters that LNER apple green should be retained, at least for a further year. One reason given for this was that the centenary celebrations for Scotland's Forth Bridge were being lined up for March 1990 and, although not the first choice, it was nevertheless the standby locomotive for participation in this event. The commemorative trains were expected to see 'A4' No 60009 *Union of South Africa* as the star locomotive, and in the event, this is what happened, but for 'political' reasons the 'Streak' was renamed *Osprey* at this time.

No 4472, as it still was, made a welcome return to the British main line on 2 May 1990 when it worked the 'FSS Executive' from Didcot to Banbury. Prior to departure a ceremony was held to unveil a plaque on the locomotive which commemorated the incredible achievement in working the world's longest nonstop run for steam traction while in Australia; 422 miles 7.59 chains from Parkes to Broken Hill. Present for the event were Dr John Prideaux, BR InterCity Director and David Evans, Deputy High Commissioner for Australia.

NORTH WALES TRAGEDY AND SEVERN VALLEY JUBILEE

Later that same month, the locomotive worked a further series of 'Sellafield Sightseer' trains, for which it was temporarily based at Carnforth before moving on to Crewe. From there it was to work a series of excursions along the North Wales coast to Holyhead, the first of which was on 16 June. On Wednesday, 18 July a dreadful tragedy occurred during the return working. As the train entered Penmaenbach Tunnel near Conwy one of the passengers was leaning out of a carriage window and his head struck the wall of the tunnel, killing him instantly. Upon arrival at Llandudno Junction, which was a scheduled stop, the carriage, where the unfortunate passenger lay, was removed from the train for forensic examination. After a 2hr delay, the train continued on its way to Crewe, the passengers needless to say, in a sombre mood. A direct consequence of this unfortunate accident was that all coaching stock used on steam-hauled excursions was fitted with window bars to prevent passengers from leaning out, and this applied for some time afterwards.

The round-the-world record breaker was still very much a main line engine but by the early 1990s the preserved steam railways had become well established as major tourist attractions, so guest appearances were beginning to feature as important items in the itinerary. One such was the Severn Valley Railway's 25th anniversary celebrations in 1990. The visit to the line eventually spread out to five weekends, from 22 September to 21 October, the first being the 'Silver Jubilee Steam Spectacular' with no less than 10 other main line engines featured, but No 4472 was billed as the star attraction in all advertising. It paid off too, with even more people than anticipated attending the event. All trains were filled and record receipts were taken.

The Severn Valley was host to *Flying Scotsman* the following autumn too but this time it had a competitor regarding one of its claims to fame. Also on this premier steam line during September and October was GWR 4-4-0

No 4472 on the BR main line, on 20 October 1991, heading a 'WA&GN Express'. *M. J. F. Bowyer*

No 3440 *City of Truro* — the locomotive that was almost certainly the first to reach 100mph, back in 1904, but not so authentically recorded as the 'A3's' achievement of 1934. To have two claimants for such a title together on the same railway was a rare privilege.

As 1992 approached rumours began to circulate that the locomotive was for sale. Such an idea was promptly scotched by Sir William but his statement included a remark that everything had its price. He added that his main concern was that, whilst he was not immortal, this locomotive was, and he wanted to ensure that it would continue in good hands. Looming up was the expiry on 27 November of the locomotive's seven-year main line certificate which would necessitate a major, and very expensive, overhaul.

LAST DAYS ON THE MAIN LINE

There were still a few months of main line activity ahead though and this included working the highly prestigious 'Royal Scotsman' luxury train over the Settle & Carlisle route. For these duties No 4472 was based on the Keighley & Worth Valley Railway in Yorkshire, a line it has rarely visited because of weight restrictions. The only time prior to this had been in 1980 when it had been featured in a television commercial for Hovis.

Flying Scotsman might not have been for sale at this time but the

Top:
Nearing Baron Wood with a southbound 'Cumbrian Mountain Express', 12 September 1992. *Hugh Ballantyne*

Above:
An earlier view, dated 20 February 1980, when No 4472 made a rare visit to the weight-restricted Keighley & Worth Valley Railway, on that occasion for filming at Keighley station. *Gavin Morrison*

spare tender was. This had not been used for a number of years as watering facilities were more readily available again because of the increase in the number of steam excursions, and so it could be released. It was sold to the A1 Locomotive Project (now a Trust) as the first step towards their ambitious and highly commendable proposal to build an entirely new Peppercorn-design LNER Pacific, which today, is in an advanced stage of construction at Darlington. The tender was acquired for the frame, wheels and fittings only, as the corridor tank was not the type required and, as it was to be fitted with roller bearing axle-boxes, these were retained as spares for the 'A3'. (It will be a historic day when *Flying Scotsman* and the new No 60163 *Tornado* meet up.)

The last main line working for what, in the event, turned out to be more than 6½ years, took place on 25 October 1992. The train ran from Ealing Broadway to Stratford-upon-Avon and return. The overhaul was not planned to take place immediately as the locomotive was considered to be fit enough for working on privately owned railways. So an intensive one-year tour of Britain's steam lines was arranged, starting with a visit to the Birmingham Railway Museum at Tyseley from the day following its BR finale.

THE GREAT RAILWAY TOUR

In order that the various steam railways should have an opportunity to share the very considerable commercial advantage of having this locomotive present, a meeting was held in Birmingham on 13 August. This was organised by Bernard Staite, the Managing Director of Flying Scotsman Services. As well as arranging who could have the locomotive and when, there was also the question of terms and conditions for such a valuable exhibit. The Keighley & Worth Valley had to decline the invitation to participate because of that weight problem, and one other line failed to respond, but the others, perhaps amazingly, were able to agree very quickly when they wanted it as each suggested different dates. The terms were accepted by all: a standard monthly charge plus £4 a mile run, the expenses of an FSS representative when in steam, and road haulage costs to be divided equally regardless of the distances involved. Such was the degree of co-operation by everyone concerned that a further season of such visits was a possibility for the future, although FSS favoured a full 10-year overhaul for a return to the main line to take place in 1994. The adoption at that time of BR Brunswick green, the BR number, double chimney and smoke deflectors was highly likely on this occasion. On paper, things were looking most promising for the future and an interesting time lay ahead.

A new dimension for the sojourn at Tyseley was that loco driving courses would be available. Therefore, for the first time in its history, literally *anyone* could take the regulator of the world's most famous locomotive. Today, footplate experience courses are a regular and highly lucrative part of the preserved railway scene, but as recently as the early 1990s they were in their infancy. What a way to attract participants and publicise such courses! These 2hr sessions were priced at £95 and soon proved extremely popular.

The Great Central Railway in Leicestershire was next to have the services of the Gresley Pacific where it joined another former Eastern Region 4-6-2, the now unique 'A2' class No 60532 *Blue Peter*. This is another locomotive with a huge following, particularly among young television viewers, once again, thanks to having the 'right' name. The Christmas period is a very busy time for steam railways with Santa specials and *Flying Scotsman* was pressed into service on Christmas Day whilst at Loughborough. The next railway to be visited was the East Lancashire Railway, one of the newer lines in the 'first division' of steam railways. They had come into the queue to have their turn at hosting the locomotive after the August agreement and had to 'make do' with a February visit, probably the quietest month of the year. The 'A3' is always a draw, so it was considered this was better than nothing and if anything could help February receipts, this would. But how lucky they were!

LLANGOLLEN DISAPPOINTMENT

The next port of call was the Llangollen Railway in Wales. This was one of those lines that had been a slow starter. The station at Llangollen is one of the most delightfully situated anywhere, right alongside the fast flowing River Dee, close to the town centre and clearly visible from the bridge that crosses the river at this point. For many years though, the line had rather struggled to get established and ran only a short distance with trains hauled by little industrial tank engines. It was not top of every enthusiast's list of places to visit by any means, but persistence had paid off. The line was extending and main line locomotives were now a regular feature.

In fact, the Llangollen Railway had quite clearly moved up into the next league, so a visit by the 'world's most famous locomotive' was a particularly important occasion for the line. It not only demonstrated that the railway was now sufficiently well established to host such a star locomotive, but was also a public statement that the Llangollen Railway was now a major player in the tourist railway market. In anticipation of the big event, extensive advertising was widely placed which featured an illustration of No 4472 prominently. In addition to working trains on all four weekends in March, weekday footplate experience courses were to be available at £95 per head for three applicants at a time. Private charter and school trains were also on offer. On Saturday evenings and Sunday lunchtimes the railway's prestigious 'Berwyn Belle' dining train would be hauled by *Flying Scotsman*, so an eventful and busy month was anticipated with all available volunteers being called on to help.

Much preparation was undertaken on the line, then 5½ miles in length, with some of the track needing to be upgraded with heavier rail and the decking on one of the bridges strengthened. With transport costs and hire charges it was stated by the railway that extra takings had to be about £5,000, just to break even. As a bonus, it was proposed to use the presence of the locomotive to launch the Llangollen Railway Society as a public limited company. The best laid plans, they say...

The LNER Pacific duly arrived at Llangollen on schedule, on 4 March, having been conveyed by road transport from the East Lancashire Railway at Bury following their highly successful month with the engine. A couple of hours after off-loading in the yard at Llangollen a routine boiler inspection was carried out, just to make sure all was in order. But, almost unbelievably, it was discovered that 25 of the 43 superheater flue tubes were leaking and there was no question of putting the locomotive in steam. Its tour of the preserved railways was cancelled on the spot! A formal letter of apology, explaining the situation was sent to the railway, as well as the other railways due to receive the locomotive later in the season. This included the assurance that Llangollen would have the first option to host the locomotive again following major repair. It appeared that work undertaken on the Great Central and East Lancashire railways to reduce smaller leaks had adversely affected the other tubes. Nobody was really to blame for what had happened, it is just one of the many problems that can be encountered with steam engines.

The locomotive remained at Llangollen as a static exhibit until the beginning of April and was still a big draw for the railway. Just to *see Flying Scotsman*, and be photographed standing by it is an attraction in itself. The overhaul was to be undertaken by FKI Babcock Robey Ltd of Oldbury, West Midlands as their bid to do the job was the most favourable — they made an unsolicited offer to replace all the superheater flue tubes free of charge. This would otherwise have cost something like £20,000 — and you can't get a much more 'favourable' quote than that!

A WHOLE NEW IMAGE

In addition to the flue tubes the 121 small tubes were also replaced, as was the smokebox. The work was completed remarkably quickly with an official roll-out on 22 July. The boiler was now insured for a further 12 months and confirmation was made that the tour of steam railways would continue into

1994. But what a surprise when No 60103 appeared. Yes, No 60103 — in fully lined BR Brunswick green livery, with double chimney and Kylchap blastpipe, *and* the German-style smoke deflectors. It looked magnificent, and so different to how everyone was expecting, despite the rumours, after 30 years in LNER apple green as No 4472.

The instigator of the change, not just in appearance but undoubtedly in the efficiency of it as a working machine, was Chief Engineer, Roland Kennington. He had been advocating the improved exhaust system for some time and he had at last managed to persuade Sir William McAlpine to allow this to be done. He had relented on the understanding that this transformation was only for while it was

A close-up of one of the German-style smoke deflectors received during the locomotive's 1993 overhaul and showing the plate stating 'Restored to final BR condition through the generosity of FKI Babcock Robey Limited'. *Author*

Left:
Now No 60103 again, *Flying Scotsman* approaches Goodrington Sands station in August 1993 when it visited the Paignton & Dartmouth Steam Railway. *Author*

off the main line and the full overhaul would see it back in familiar apple green again. Roland had had the blastpipe assembly made up a few years before and had obtained the original plans for the smoke deflectors from the National Railway Museum, so all that had been outstanding was the chimney. He then heard that there was one of these in an enthusiast's garden. This particular garden must be well known to many rail travellers on the Waterloo-West of England route as it is clearly visible alongside the up line at Worting Junction, just west of Basingstoke, and is *full* of railwayana, particularly station nameboards. The owner of the chimney, Ron Grace, has allowed it to be borrowed for as long as it is required for use on the locomotive.

The first public appearance of the locomotive in its new guise was a visit to the Paignton & Dartmouth Steam Railway, a line it had been to before, a number of years earlier. The importance this locomotive holds within the railway enthusiast fraternity was then amply demonstrated. There were those writing to say how absolutely thrilled they were to see what they described as 'a proper' 'A3' class locomotive again, in the style and livery that they remembered them, this including the author it should be said. Then there were those who were horrified by what they said was the 'sacrilege' of desecrating this *LNER* Pacific! The volume of correspondence in the railway press expressing the view one way or the other was unprecedented. It is a debate that will go on indefinitely, but all seem to accept the fact that the choice of liveries lies between these two alternatives. Had the locomotive fallen into different hands to those of today, commercial sponsorship may by now have been playing its part in the livery carried. Can *Flying Scotsman* ever be imagined in the 'house' colours of a multinational company, such as all over gold, scarlet with a young lady trailing a union flag motif, or even black and white stripes? I think perhaps we should be grateful that we are able to confine the debate to the shade of green to be adopted!

SCOTSMAN, McALPINE AND WATERMAN

A change of ownership did occur only a couple of months after the overhaul when Sir William McAlpine's company joined forces on 21 September 1993 with a much newer organisation, Waterman Railways. Waterman Railways had risen meteorically to establish itself as one of the first companies to become actively involved in the rail privatisation process by acquiring British Rail's Special Trains Service. It was really a one-man company, that of the 'hit man', pop music entrepreneur Pete Waterman. He has had an interesting and varied life, but a true and accurate account has yet to be written. It is believed he left school at an early age and

Above:
A well-known and very successful record producer, Pete Waterman became part-owner of *Flying Scotsman* with Sir William McAlpine when they combined forces in September 1993. He is seen here, right, at Old Oak Common open day, 19 March 1994 with Capital Radio DJ, Richard Allinson (now of BBC Radio 2), at the naming of Class 47 diesel No 47366, *Capital Radio's Help a London Child. Author*

worked as a fitter's apprentice at Wolverhampton Stafford Road shed which is where he got his taste for railways. Various involvements in the entertainment industry, and the pop music business in particular, ultimately led to him teaming up with a couple of song writers, Mike Stock and Matt Aitken. From that point on things are much better recorded, in more ways than one. The credit 'Stock, Aitken & Waterman' became one of the most successful in recorded music history with an almost total and unique domination of the pop charts for a number of years. Their first No 1 hit was *You Spin Me Around (Like a Record)* by the group Dead or Alive, which entered the charts in March 1985 on the Epic label. Over the next few years they produced more than 100 records that reached the charts, over half of which made the top 10. They were probably best known for their hits with Kylie Minogue, Jason Donovan and Rick Astley, but long-established artists like Cliff Richard were queueing up to be recorded by them. Pete Waterman also formed his own, very successful record label, PWL, but like so many pop music relationships, that with Stock and Aitken ended in acrimony and dispute.

Pete Waterman's personal interest appeared to be modern traction, diesel and electric locomotives, and starting with a Class 25 he accumulated an amazing collection of representative examples. Several classes of locomotive could quite well be extinct today but for his timely acquisitions. He has also amassed a very large collection of railwayana and model steam locomotives, with most classes of his two favourite railways represented — the Great Western and London & North Western.

One railway he had never been particularly interested in was the LNER. However, when the opportunity arose to become a half owner of the world's most famous locomotive, this was considered too good an opportunity to miss, and the two companies appeared, at first, to slot together well. As he later said, 'Any locomotive which has sufficient charisma that you can sell pieces of coal off the tender at two quid a time, has got to have something going for it!'

No 60103 makes a fine sight as it crosses the River Dee, shortly after leaving Llangollen station with the 16.15 to Glyndyfrdwy on 20 March during its 1994 visit to the Llangollen Railway.
John S. Whiteley

THE 1994 TOUR

Throughout 1994 No 60103 continued its tour of steam railways and centres with the Birmingham Railway Museum at Tyseley, securing a deal with the new management structure for an exclusive right to footplate experience courses with the engine from October to December each year until 1998, but as it turned out this was not able to be put into practice.

During the spring the promised return to the Llangollen Railway was made, this time in full working order of course. The early summer was spent on the Nene Valley Railway which had missed out the previous year, then late summer saw the locomotive on the Swanage Railway in Dorset. This was another line like the Llangollen. It had been many years getting established but had recently moved up into the big time as a tourist attraction, too quickly in fact. A major extension to the track had been made but due to planning restrictions it had not been possible to reopen this section to fare-paying passengers and further extension to a new station, better situated for road access, was required. The result was near financial disaster, possibly coming as close to collapse as any steam railway has yet.

New management, severe cost cutting and other drastic measures — plus the pulling power of *Flying Scotsman* — saved the day. The railway admitted that the enormous attraction of this locomotive had boosted passenger receipts to new levels and had contributed significantly to their financial recovery. This was despite the aforementioned rumours about the locomotive's authenticity as it had the 'wrong' number and was not the right green, and besides, someone was heard to say, 'What is such a famous train (sic) doing in our part of the country anyway?' The locomotive had now become so famous it not only had the possibility of being impersonated but some people could not really believe their eyes when they did see it!

The Severn Valley Railway was the next railway to be graced by the Gresley Pacific, again making up for the aborted 1993 visit. It was then back to the Birmingham Railway Museum for its annual driver training commitment which proved to be as popular as ever.

LLANGOLLEN FINALE

The 1995 tour of preserved railways was confirmed as being 'definitely the last season', starting the year at Llangollen again. This railway was now highly organised in its utilisation of the locomotive with a very full and interesting programme of events lined up. Local businesses were also benefiting from the presence of this crowd-puller in their town. From 12 January to late April, the following trains were scheduled to be worked on the Llangollen Railway on the days advertised:

- The 'Berwyn Belle'. A prestigious dining train operated over the entire reopened section of line from Llangollen to Glyndyfrdwy.
- The 'Mid-day Belle'. Also a dining train serving a traditional three-course roast Sunday lunch.
- The 'Evening Belle'. A double-journey train to Glyndyfrdwy departing from Llangollen at 19.30, with four-course dinner served.
- The 'Burns Night Belle'. Run on the evening of Saturday, 28 January to the skirl o' the pipes with entertainment between dinner courses of readings from Robert Burns's work.
- The 'Musical Belle'. As the 'Evening Belle' but on 11 March with musical accompaniment in the form of a jazz band with dancing in the function car *Gwenabwy* during a stop at Berwyn station. 22 April was similar but the music was classical.
- The 'Murder on the Berwyn Belle'. Probably the most novel train of all. Passengers were encouraged to dress in Edwardian costume and were greeted on arrival by a master of ceremonies. After boarding the train a dastardly plot unfolded as a group of actors and actresses performed a whodunnit. The passengers then had to participate in collecting clues and accuse the suspects, a three-course meal being served throughout the evening.
- The 'Sixties Belle'. One night only, 8 April, as the 'Musical Belle' but to the sounds of the Merseybeat and with the passengers wearing winkle-pickers, paisley ties and knitted mini dresses.
- The 'Night Scotsman'. The final train in the original programme, on 29 April, with passengers joining in the chorus of 'Auld Lang Syne' as a 'farewell to *Flying Scotsman*', but this one was not to be.

In addition to this very full programme of passenger trains there was also an intensive series of driver training courses. The draw of such a famous locomotive on this most scenic of lines even attracted enthusiasts from abroad. One participant came from Switzerland while Australian tycoon, Sir Eric Neal, made a special flight to the UK in order to take his place to drive the first train hauled by the engine on this visit to the railway. Aged 71, he was the Chairman of Westpac, a very large banking organisation as well as being Chairman of Coca Cola (Australia) and BICC Cables (Australia). Such an enthusiastic visitor gave the railway some valuable publicity when the media picked up on the event.

The sole-surviving 'A3' Pacific made a return visit to the Llangollen Railway in 1995 and is seen ready to depart from Llangollen station on 5 March with the 'Mid-day Belle'. The locomotive had to be taken out of traffic the following month while on this railway, and was not to be seen in steam again for more than four years. *Author*

As for the engine's previous visit to the Llangollen Railway, extensive advertising was placed specifically for these events. This time, the then topical catch phrase, 'It Could be *You!*' was used, this referring to the fact that for £199 *you* could drive *Flying Scotsman* yourself, with full tuition and safety instruction. This was possibly going to be the last chance anyone would have of such an experience this century as once the locomotive had had its next major overhaul it would be returning to the main line for much of the time and simply would not be so readily available for the 'amateur' driver.

Even before arrival in Wales on 11 January, many bookings had been received for the footplate experience courses and the locomotive was in action at every available opportunity as yet more people applied. The stay on the line was scheduled for 16 weeks but in late April, just at the end of this period, things began to go wrong following 15 highly successful weeks of operation. First, a slow-speed derailment occurred near Llangollen station while the engine was working empty coaching stock. No damage was sustained by this extremely heavy locomotive but external assistance was required in re-railing as all wheels were off the track. Staff called over from Rail Express Systems at Crewe Depot came with appropriate lifting tackle and soon had the *Scotsman* back on the metals the following morning.

Then, on Sunday, 23 April steam was noticed entering the cab and this was traced to the top right-hand shoulder of the firebox. It was taken out of traffic there and then. A couple of days later a boiler inspector declared the locomotive 'unfit to steam' and so Roland Kennington arranged transport back to Southall with a view to the heavy general overhaul starting as soon as possible. This meant that the proposed summer visit to the Paignton & Dartmouth Steam Railway would have to be cancelled.

It was at this point that cracks also began to appear within the locomotive's team. Part owner, Pete Waterman, issued a statement that the Devon visit was *not* going to be cancelled because the firebox could be patched up by means of welding so that the locomotive could continue in service for the remainder of the season to see out its boiler certificate which expired in October.

However, the return to the locomotive's London base was to be made after all. The 'A3' was conveyed by road to Brentford and was then diesel-hauled along the freight-only branch to Southall Depot where the work would take place.

4472

7 AS GOOD AS NEW FOR THE NEW MILLENNIUM

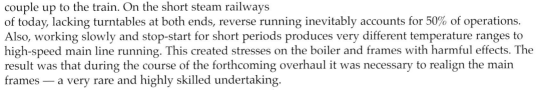

Flying Scotsman arrived at the owner's Southall depot on 9 June 1995 following its failure at Llangollen but few could have predicted just how long it would be before re-emergence from the works would take place. The owners had recently undergone changes in their administrative organisation. As from 1 April Flying Scotsman Services and Pete Waterman's Special Trains Unit ceased to exist and Flying Scotsman Railways became the parent company of the group. The train operating company took the name Waterman Railways with this branding to be used although the assets, including locomotives, rolling stock and workshops, were to be the property of the Carriage and Traction Company. Pete Waterman was appointed Chief Executive with Ron Cadman as Managing Director. Sir William McAlpine was on the board of directors of the various companies. The future appeared positive, especially as it was stated that ex-BR staff were to be included in the organisation particularly in respect of operating and engineering and that consultants were to be appointed to include representatives from the railway enthusiast market.

Despite all the good intentions, the cracks in the organisation were to prove even more difficult to patch up than those in the locomotive's firebox. Flying Scotsman's Chief Engineer, Roland Kennington, declared the firebox could not be instantly repaired and commenced preparatory work for a major overhaul. The boiler lift was to take place in late June but first a 10-ton A-frame lifting gantry had to be constructed in the works. The German smoke deflectors, smokebox door, cab and boiler fittings were removed as the first step towards complete dismantling in readiness for what turned out to be the most thorough overhaul of its life, and probably of any locomotive in preservation, costing more than any other too.

One of the reasons for such an extensive renovation being called for was said to be the amount of time it had spent performing duties for which it was not 'designed' — and something it would not be subjected to again to the same degree in the future. The extended period of time on the preserved railways and at steam centres, which had included 'driver experience courses', had taken its toll. This was not the fault of the railways, or the amateur drivers who were of course working under strict, expert supervision at all times, but the nature of the locomotive's workings. The 'A' classes of Pacifics were designed by Nigel Gresley for continuous, long-distance running — forwards. Reverse running was only ever done occasionally or at slow speed in shed yards or into the station to couple up to the train. On the short steam railways of today, lacking turntables at both ends, reverse running inevitably accounts for 50% of operations. Also, working slowly and stop-start for short periods produces very different temperature ranges to high-speed main line running. This created stresses on the boiler and frames with harmful effects. The result was that during the course of the forthcoming overhaul it was necessary to realign the main frames — a very rare and highly skilled undertaking.

A visit to Flying Scotsman Railways' depot at Southall in September 1995 found the locomotive basically complete, but with major work stopped. *Author*

95

DISAGREEMENTS IN THE CAMP

Such an extensive restoration would inevitably take a lot of time and money but not everyone within the organisation could understand why a timescale of something like two or more years for being out of action and more importantly, away from revenue-earning service, was necessary. As early as September 1995, the national press had picked up on the fact that this famous engine was going to be out of the public eye for some considerable time to come. Meanwhile, some members of staff were having to be laid off due to problems encountered with BR's subsidiaries with which the train operating division was having to deal. This was put down to the fact that they were rail privatisation pioneers and were finding out just what this meant! Not long after this, Waterman Railways had to pull out of running main line steam charter trains because of the excessive costs being imposed by the still-nationalised railway network. The future for main line steam was beginning to look bleak indeed, and the long-term future of *Flying Scotsman*, destined for this market, was becoming precarious from a financial point of view. The whole climate of privately owned steam locomotives operating on the main line was changing — quickly

The author visited Southall one Sunday morning in early September to find out just what was happening, if anything, as there were so many conflicting stories about the situation. He had already been contacted by one of the owners with the suggestion that a book should be produced as it had been such a long time since anything had been published covering the full history of the locomotive. While agreeing that this was a worthwhile venture the uncertainty of when she would be seen in steam again meant it was impossible to set a publishing date but a date of 1999/2000 was certainly not in mind at that time!

Upon arrival at Southall a visit was made first to the GWR Preservation Group who were then tenants of the main shed with a large collection of locomotives and rolling stock. The lone volunteer present asked if I had heard the 'news'. When I enquired what this might be he simply said, *'Flying Scotsman* — it's all finished!'. 'Good grief! They must have really pulled out all the stops' was my reply, although I suspected what he really meant of course. He then amplified his remark by saying how sad it was that the locomotive was now destined to languish in the works for the foreseeable future, the paid staff had been laid off, the volunteers instructed not to carry out any work requiring expenditure and that the organisation had in effect collapsed. He was not to know at that stage just how significant the change of circumstances would be regarding their own establishment. It is another story, but the GWR Preservation Group were subsequently forced to vacate the site at Southall following the later change of *Flying Scotsman*'s ownership but, after a very difficult period, have found new and hopefully ideal London premises at Strawberry Hill.

A visit to the Flying Scotsman Railway (FSR) works which lay beyond the main shed, found the locomotive basically intact but looking forlorn, although not quite as bad as the dailies would have had us believe. With various fittings removed, including the boiler cladding, it did look rather woebegone but nothing like as bad, externally at least, as the many locomotives that had been rescued from Woodham's yard at Barry over the years. There was only one person present that morning who had come in after being away on holiday. He was not sure what had happened but all he knew was that no further work was to be undertaken on the locomotive without direct authorisation from the owners.

IN LIMBO

Little more was heard over the next couple of months, other than circulating rumours regarding the financial health of the *Flying Scotsman* organisation, until early 1996 when a report was published with the headline: 'NatWest Bank lays claim to ownership of *Flying Scotsman*'. From this it appeared that the bank had claimed a legal right to the locomotive in lieu of a large debt owed to them by Waterman Railways. This interest was declared by the placing of a plate on one of the cab-side steps. However, Pete Waterman quickly reacted by explaining that it was not true the bank 'owned' the locomotive but it had been used as a guarantee against a bank loan and it meant no more than the fact that the loan would have to be repaid before the locomotive was ever sold. The magazine subsequently apologised for the wrong impression their report may have given regarding the ownership of the locomotive or the financial state of affairs of the companies involved but such an item once published, tends to stick in the mind. Nevertheless, the incident brought the locomotive into the limelight even when it was out of sight in a locked shed.

In fact, all the time it was out of action it was never long before one of the national dailies had a feature, even if not entirely accurate or complimentary in their reporting. Today, there are so many other magnificent steam locomotives at work restored by enthusiasts, many from scrapyard condition that are hauling trains on the main lines the length and breadth of Britain yet are never considered newsworthy by the media at large. It is therefore all the more remarkable how the mystique of Alan Pegler's purchase has permeated through to today's media.

A *Daily Mail* colour feature on 2 March 1996 stated how the massive maintenance costs had left it 'sidelined and forgotten'. But judging by the national press one would be forgiven for thinking this was the only steam locomotive to have survived and one that was certainly never forgotten! The joint owners of the locomotive were only too aware of the situation in which they found themselves; custodians of the world's most famous, and loved, locomotive, but restricted in how they could progress matters due to the huge finances required with any financial return from main line operation looking dubious.

Sir William McAlpine, who had owned the locomotive for nearly as many years as did the LNER, was now prepared to consider relinquishing his share if this meant a better future for it. The suggestion of a publicly owned trust had been put forward and such a possibility was being investigated. Nick Pigott, the editor of *The Railway Magazine*, is well-known for his enthusiasm for Gresley's 'A1/A3' Pacifics and devoted the magazine's editorial in the March issue to backing such a proposal, going as far as to offer to contribute personally to any such fund set up.

Messrs McAlpine and Waterman stated that not only were they not immortal but the future of the engine was far more important than their continued ownership. Elsewhere in the same issue of the magazine, the 'Hit man' went further by saying he was 'totally fed up' with the politics of railway privatisation and wanted nothing more to do with running Waterman Railways. This was to lead to him selling many of his large fleet of diesel and electric locomotives and an apparent return to concentrating on the music industry. He felt he had been neglecting this side of his business due to his railway involvements of late and that it was an ever-changing scene that needed full attention to keep up with the trends. Today, he is again heavily involved in the railway scene, both commercially and as a 'hobby' and his presence in the pop charts has since been reinstated with the likes of Steps, one of the most successful pop acts of the late 1990s.

ENTER THE DOCTOR

In early 1996 negotiations for the sale of *Flying Scotsman* were taking place although few details were being released other than the categoric statement that restoration would definitely be completed in time for the millennium — then still four years away. The Pacific was stated to be worth £1.25 million.

Then, the announcement was made; the 1 March issue of the weekly *Steam Railway News* carrying the story that No 4472 had been acquired by Oxford businessman Tony Marchington. The purchase included the support coach, a sleeping car and the complete Metro-Cammell-built Pullman car train, along with the maintenance equipment at the Southall depot as well as the name of Flying Scotsman Railways Ltd. Full restoration to main line status was to commence immediately but this was to be thorough and the job was not to be rushed in order to meet a deadline by skimping on any aspect, although an initial target for completion and entry into service was given as 1 May 1998. This would mark the 70th anniversary of the first nonstop run from King's Cross to Edinburgh. Roland Kennington, who had been laid off in late 1995, was reappointed and would be fully responsible for the locomotive's restoration and subsequent maintenance.

Dr Tony Marchington was, until this time, better known within the traction engine fraternity than among railway enthusiasts but this was about to change. Ten years earlier, as a member of the Buxworth Steam Group in Derbyshire, he had organised a huge and memorable steam event at Lyme Park near Stockport, the star guest being Fred Dibnah, the Bolton steeplejack of television fame who was there with the present author signing their latest book. The slim, young Tony Marchington will always be remembered for appearing to be everywhere on site all at once ensuring everyone was where they were supposed to be and that they had all their requirements met. Definitely a case of dynamic hands-on management!

Dr Marchington had launched his company in 1979 and has obviously worked at this with similar expertise and enthusiasm, with Oxford Molecular Group PLC, of which he is now Chief Executive, being floated on the Stock Exchange in 1994. This raised £30 million but the company was only a short while later valued at £200 million.

On Friday, 23 February 1996 the deal was finalised when the 40-year-old millionaire shook hands with Sir William McAlpine. The final sale agreement was signed at Southall on 6 March for a figure reputed to be £1.5 million. Needless to say, such dramatic news was seized upon by the railway press and national media alike with every railway magazine featuring 'exclusive' interviews with the future owner. This made an interesting comparison with the coverage afforded Alan Pegler when he bought the locomotive from British Railways back in 1963 for £3,000 — and in full working order. The national press had picked up on it as a good news story, but the few railway titles of the time barely gave it a mention, one not until a couple of months after the event. The magazines were all a lot quicker off the mark this time!

Many of the comments made by Tony Marchington in those early interviews are of interest when analysed three years later, especially when bearing in mind that a May 1998 completion had been hoped for.

As well as announcing that a supporters' organisation would be formed — the Flying Scotsman Association — came suggestions of nonstop runs between London and Edinburgh, £2,000 fares and a millennium special leaving King's Cross on 31 December 1999 and returning after an overnight stop in Scotland on 1 January 2000. Also, there were no plans for the locomotive to go on any overseas visits while in his ownership — and it would be finished in Brunswick green livery as No 60103.

When the Flying Scotsman Association was launched in the summer of 1996 it was most fitting and pleasing that Alan Pegler was made President, thus re-establishing his links with the 'old girl'. A direct benefit of this appointment was that he would be entitled to unlimited free travel behind 'his' locomotive again. Another well-known railway name to join the *Flying Scotsman* team at this time was David Ward, a former director of BR InterCity's Special Trains Unit who became an honorary consultant and now holds the position of Operations Manager. He is also a trustee of the Bressingham Steam Museum in Norfolk. Among that collection's superb range of exhibits is the 15in gauge fine scale model of No 4472 built by Bill Stewart which has been confined to static display for many years. To coincide with the return to operation of the 'real thing' this too has received a thorough overhaul including a new boiler and was steamed again in mid 1999. The possibilities of the two locomotives, identical in every respect except size, being seen together is an intriguing prospect.

The serious job of restoring the full-size locomotive was soon got underway with Roland Kennington as the the only full-time member of the engineering team, but assisted by a dedicated and skilled group of nine regular volunteers. The sudden change in the locomotive's fortune was welcome and exciting news which came as a relief as much as anything to its many 'fans' around the world.

General interest in this famous locomotive was now as high as ever and this possibly reflected in an auction room sale of a Terence Cuneo painting on 10 September 1996. This was the original painting depicting *Flying Scotsman* on the Forth Bridge and was from Sir William McAlpine's personal collection. It was expected to fetch about £6,000 but on the day frantic bidding took the price up to £26,000 — the highest price ever paid for an original Cuneo which was the first to go on sale following the artist's death at the beginning of the year.

It is not the intention to describe in detail the work undertaken during this overhaul as this has been reported as it progressed in the railway press and was so thorough that a full description would make a fascinating book in itself, especially as every stage was covered by a professional photographer. Most of the work was undertaken on site at Southall under the personal supervision of Roland Kennington but some items were subcontracted out including the boiler which went to Chatham Steam Ltd, Kent for major attention. The aim was for the locomotive to be even *better* than when newly built. While keeping everything as original as possible modern technology was to be employed wherever this could be of

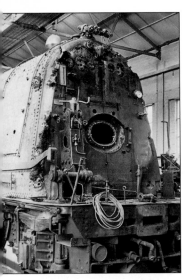

assistance in improving the efficiency in the work undertaken. An example of this is the three crosshead castings — a critical link between the cylinders and the driving wheels. Measuring 18in x 12in these were cast by a company in Huddersfield who are confident that their precision work will ensure the locomotive will run with improved coal and water consumption.

THE LIVERY CONTROVERSY, AGAIN

While all this intense activity was underway enthusiasts were now able to sit back confident that this superb machine would be available for them to travel behind and photograph again sometime fairly soon. Almost inevitably, the closer it got to completion the more their attention returned to the old chestnut of its livery and again this began to be debated in the railway magazines. What really fanned the flames of debate was when it was indicated that the locomotive was expected to be finished in apple green livery as LNER No 4472, but it was going to be fitted with a double chimney and Kylchap blastpipe. This combination of livery and chimney was declared 'unauthentic' and what added further to the controversy was the opinion expressed by many that it would also need to have the BR-era German-style smoke deflectors — these and LNER green?!

The volunteers working on the restoration nearly all wanted to see completion in Brunswick green as No 60103 but the new owner favoured an apple green No 4472, not least because he knew that most people had come to know the engine in this guise both in this country and around the world. The argument that this livery was not historically correct no longer applied as it had already carried this livery for so long previously it had itself made it authentic. Engineers entered the debate by saying smoke deflectors would be essential with this exhaust arrangement as smoke drifting towards the footplate would become a safety issue. Even David Ward allowed himself to enter the fray by writing to one of the periodicals pointing out that even Brunswick green would not be 'authentic' and in fact such an aim was now impossible and that 'doing

Top:
Happy to be back at work again and restoring the engine he loves, Chief Engineer, Roland Kennington in the Southall works, February 1997. *Author*

Above:
A major task undertaken was the refurbishment and installation of a replacement middle cylinder shown standing upright for machining. *Author*

what is sensible and appropriate' is the best principle to adopt. In early 1998 a formal announcement was made that the livery would be LNER apple green and that if smoke drift did prove to be a problem when the engine was in service the German smoke deflectors would be installed. The livery decision was finally settled as it was regarded as a marketing matter — that's what the paying public, and particularly the full-dining clientele, would want to see. Alan Pegler's comment on the situation was that if the smoke deflectors did need to be fitted then perhaps they should be considered also for the double chimney GWR 'King' class locomotive!

FAME BY ASSOCIATION

Flying Scotsman did not really need such fruitless debate to keep in the news and a couple of other items appeared at this time indicating how much it had become part of the nation's consciousness. Britain's oldest man, Vinson Gulliver, then aged 109, died peacefully in a Manchester hospital on 7 August 1997. He had started his working life on the Great Central Railway in 1907 as locomotive cleaner at Trafford Park working his way up to become a driver, rising to the top link at Gorton shed in LNER days. In the final years he obtained considerable celebrity status due to his age especially as he continued in good health and even on his 108th birthday, enjoyed being treated to a front-seat ride in one of the Metrolink trams, travelling from Altrincham to Manchester and back. Following his death nearly all the published reports on his very long and active life made mention of one particular fact, and 'claim to fame' — he had driven *Flying Scotsman* and this for just the short distance into Gorton Works, Manchester for an intermediate repair when Doncaster had been too busy.

In July 1997 *The Railway Magazine* commemorated 100 years of publishing and to mark the occasion issued a limited edition postal cover. Almost inevitably, the locomotive chosen to grace this item, printed on a silken fabric, was dear old No 4472.

A party of Flying Scotsman Association members inspect the work in progress in February 1997, accompanied by David Ward, Operations Manager, right. *Author*

On Friday, 19 September 1997 the work in the Southall shed was brought to an abrupt halt with a very loud bang and a shudder. On the main line railway running through Southall station and past the works, the 10.32 Swansea-Paddington HST collided with an ARC stone train being reversed across the main line. One of the worst rail disasters of recent times, the wreckage spilled across the tracks and to within a few yards of Flying Scotsman Railways' premises which were clearly visible in the newspaper and television pictures, although few, if any, mentioned the fact.

One very important aspect of the restoration of the 4-6-2 has been the fitting of air brakes, a necessity for working trains of modern coaching stock. Several other main line steam locomotives had already been adorned with such a feature, some less well-positioned than others from an aesthetic point of view. The equipment on *Flying Scotsman* is fitted discreetly out of sight with the air pump positioned on the main frames behind the trailing driving axle and is capable of working both the locomotive brakes and the air brakes on a train.

The high cost of fitting this equipment was partly paid for by travel writer Kenneth Westcott Jones who died in April 1997 and who had bequeathed £35,000 for the 'furtherance of main line steam into the 21st century'. Other locomotives to benefit similarly were Bulleid Pacific *City of Wells* and Stanier 'Princess' *Princess Margaret Rose*. (Mr Jones did not forget the Great Western in his will, the 6024 Preservation Society receiving a similar amount towards the restoration of a tender for *King Edward I*.)

With the locomotive fast approaching its 80th anniversary and its future as bright as ever, it is inevitable that as the story unfolds deaths will enter the script from time to time, but this chapter does seem to have become unintentionally morbid so the last word on this subject goes to the commemoration of a life. The locomotive's designer, Sir Nigel Gresley, received a further honour on 24 September 1997, 56 years after his death, when English Heritage unveiled one of its blue plaques at King's Cross station. The ceremony was performed by Gresley's grandson, Tim Godfrey, and was the first such plaque to be displayed at someone's former place of work rather than a residence.

THE END IS IN SIGHT

By early 1998 it had become clear that a rapid return to steam was not going to be possible and a new date of spring 1999 was set, it being stated that the thoroughness of the work meant it was going to be a 'Rolls-Royce job'. (Was this a veiled indication that *German* smoke deflectors *were* going to be fitted?...)

The restoration has been described as the most comprehensive and costly of any British steam locomotive and although actual figures have not been released it is understood this has been something in the order of £750,000; certainly far more than originally bargained for. In January 1999, Roland Kennington gave a detailed lecture to a railway society on the work required to bring *Flying Scotsman* back to present day main line operating standards. The amount of corrosion that had taken place over the years, much of it previously undetected, had been alarming. Alan Pegler was praised for his foresight in buying a spare boiler and middle cylinder when he had had the opportunity. However, even such forward thinking had not solved all the problems of today's restoration. When it came to fitting the refurbished replacement middle cylinder it was discovered that few of the bolt holes lined up and hence nearly 200 new holes had to be reamed out.

When asked how much of the locomotive could be claimed to be original Mr Kennington came back with the speedy reply: 'None of it!' He then went on to explain that in the late 1920s, when Doncaster Works was receiving locomotives with cracked main frames, to save time in returning them to traffic these were replaced with newly fabricated frames. Furthermore, when first built, the weight of these locomotives exceeded the specified limit so the original plain frames were replaced by three-quarter frames with holes to make them lighter in weight.

Come the end of February the boiler was still awaiting return from Kent but completion was considered to be on schedule for a return to the main line for test running in late May with the first passenger workings scheduled for 5 and 12 June. The main target however was set as Sunday, 4 July to work from King's Cross up the East Coast main line to York. No 4472 would then be placed on temporary display at the National Railway Museum for the formal opening of the new, £4 million engineering workshop on the 7th. The fare for this historic occasion was set at £350 per head.

A press conference was held on Wednesday, 14 April at the Cavendish Hotel in London announcing the imminent completion of restoration and the return to main line operation. A press release was issued together with an elaborate 16-page full-colour brochure giving details of 15 trains from 4 July to the end of the year, century — and millennium — 4,000 train seats being available. Destinations included York, Salisbury Norwich, Stratford-upon-Avon and Edinburgh, all starting from London except that on 11 July which would see the engine returning from its week-long stay at York. Fares started at £200 per person, rising to £2000 for the 'Millenium Scotsman'.

As previously promised however, members of the Association were to be given the opportunity to travel behind 'their' locomotive before the commencement of this programme, and at a 'reduced' fare. Consequently it was announced that a train primarily for FSA members would be run on Saturday, 26 June departing from Paddington working to Worcester via Birmingham and returning via Evesham. For this the fare was set at £125 first class and £75 standard class for members, with bookings made available as from 5 May to the general public charged at the same rate as guests of members, £145 and £95 respectively. In the event however, such fares did not prove sufficiently tempting and this, the first scheduled train behind the newly restored *Flying Scotsman* was cancelled due to insufficient support, with members allowed a discount on the 4 July train instead.

Later the same day, following the press launch, Roland Kennington exchanged his suit and tie for his more usual attire of a boiler suit, and set to at Southall for the installation of the locomotive's boiler. Just after midnight this was

Above:
Nearly there! No 4472, as it is again, almost complete but in grey primer, at Southall on the occasion of the first official photo call since restoration, 27 May 1999. *Chris Milner*

Right:
The proud and happy owner, Dr Tony Marchington, Southall, 27 May 1997. *Chris Milner*

lowered back into the frames and it looked like a locomotive once again. Although a letter dated 15 April was received from David Ward stating that 'there are unlikely to be any photo calls at Southall', just such an event was held in late May. The date was at first set for 21 May but this was postponed at short notice as it was decided it was inappropriate to hold a celebratory event on this day as this was to be the funeral of Jill Dando, the popular television presenter who had been murdered.

'FLYING SCOTSMAN' IS FINISHED

The new photo call date of 27 May turned out to be a beautifully sunny morning and the now fully restored Pacific was hauled out of the works by a diesel shunter. No 4472 was still in grey primer but nevertheless looked magnificent and was clearly a machine restored to perfection. There was a fire in the firebox for the first time since it had been dropped hurriedly at Llangollen more than four years earlier. The national press was out in force and, even if not immediately, most newspapers were to have extended features on the 'world's most famous locomotive' with histories of varying accuracy. While four years may appear a long time out of the public eye this should be compared with the length of time many less well-known locomotive restorations have taken and the fact that some engines lie dismantled for *decades* while work progresses, slowly but steadily. In actual fact, the three-year restoration was a remarkably speedy operation.

This was not the first occasion the locomotive was hauled out for photographs however as it was seen in daylight a couple of days earlier, albeit without smokebox door and tender attached, this being for the benefit of the *Railway Magazine* photographer as the change of date for the official photo call would have meant missing the magazine's press-date for another month!

FUTURE PLANS

Although the story is brought to a fitting conclusion with its magnificent return to the locomotive's old stamping ground, the East Coast main line, and a high profile departure from King's Cross, there is clearly going to be much more to report in the future as its fame spreads even further and new destinations are reached. For example, it has been announced that it will once again be running with two water tenders and an overseas visit might be considered. The second tender, to be built at Southall, will be painted in umber and cream to match the Pullman train which will be the eventual stock to work behind this locomotive and Tony Marchington's other Gresley Pacific, streamlined 'A4' class No 60019 *Bittern* which is currently under restoration. It is hoped this tender will be completed in time for use on the 'Millennium Scotsman' working.

IN CONCLUSION

After the years of work and dedication No 4472 was eventually completed and ready for steam trials on the main line. The first run was made under the cover of darkness, in the early hours of 22 June to Didcot and back, followed by three night-time workings, slightly further afield from Southall down to Westbury in Wiltshire and back. The final proving trial before the 'big day' took it to the West Midlands during daylight hours on Saturday, 26 June, still in grey undercoat and hauling a 10-coach set and a support vehicle as empty stock. The outward journey was via Banbury to Birmingham Snow Hill and Worcester, returning via Evesham and Oxford. Then, as planned on Sunday, 4 July, complete in its magnificent LNER apple green livery and numbered 4472 for the first time since early 1993, it slowly backed down on to its train at London, King's Cross. Present on the platform was Alan Pegler who found the occasion very emotional. It was no less than 75 years before that he had first set eyes on this magnificent locomotive, a sight he would never forget. He had seen it ready to head north from this magnificent station when he had first saved it for posterity, 36 years ago. Now, it was about to do the same, setting off on yet another new career. So much had changed in the world during those years, yet looking at this locomotive, nothing had changed. For everyone present it was a sensational sight but for Alan it brought back so many personal memories, almost as if in some ways life had come full-circle.

All those present seemed impatient to see the train set off on its historic journey — even those there to watch could not help but want to see the engine start the train and head so quickly out of view into Gasworks Tunnel. This tunnel had always given the famous terminus an almost magical quality in the days of steam when *Flying Scotsman,* and all the other famous LNER Pacifics, would arrive so suddenly and then disappear again equally quickly. Although scheduled for a 09.15 departure the train actually left at 08.55, having been re-timed to 08.52. The total weight was in excess of 500 tons which included an electric locomotive coupled to the back of the train (No 86426), 'just in case' — remember Alice Springs? It was not needed of course and merely added to the burden and the locomotive performed as expected — magnificently. The 10-coach train was the Mk 1 set of carriages, 'Pride of the Nation' and was filled with about 250 passengers and departed to the sound of bagpipes. The route was lined with thousands of excited well-wishers who greeted an old friend as it passed by. After a water stop at Peterborough the famed Stoke Bank was tackled with the speed being maintained at a creditable 52mph. Arrival at York was 15min down, but this was not attributable to the locomotive's performance in any way, and the return to operation was deemed a 100% success with little apparent problem with drifting smoke.

Already it is difficult to imagine the locomotive as *not* being available to see and experience, just as for a few years it had become hard to envisage when it would be back in action again. A heartfelt 'thanks' and congratulations are due to Dr Tony Marchington, Roland Kennington and their dedicated team for what they have achieved. When this story started to be written the closing paragraphs could in no way be predicted but no better end could have been anticipated for the story than has happened. There will be many more chapters to be added in the years to come, and who knows what these may contain?

Writing in his book, *I Tried to Run a Railway,* the late Gerard Fiennes, a BR Eastern Region Manager, stated 'Good journeys by rail have no history.' Perhaps this is true on the whole, but No 4472 *Flying Scotsman* is the exception as *every* time it turns its wheels it is making history, and long may it do so.

Once again on main line service, No 4472 is seen being admired by onlookers at Salisbury on 25 July 1999. This was the first of four 'Sarum Scotsman' workings made between then and 5 September 1999. *Author*

D uring its working life, *Flying Scotsman* was not a unique locomotive and the accompanying list shows its relationship with other locomotives of its type. *Flying Scotsman* was the third of the 52 'A1' class 4-6-2s to be built, albeit the first locomotive to be completed by the newly formed LNER in 1923. Following its upgrading with a higher pressure boiler in 1947 it became one of no less than 78 Class A3s which were numbered 60035 to 60112 inclusive. In such a list, when numbered 60103, *Flying Scotsman* assumes a certain degree of anonymity. Previously, in 1945, the first 'A1' to have been built, No 4470 *Great Northern*, had been completely rebuilt by Edward Thompson, Gresley's successor on the LNER. This was then classified 'A1/1', and in consequence the 17 original 'A1s' that had not at that time been re-classified to 'A3', became Class A10 as from 25 April 1945. This included No 4472.

The following is a basic listing of all the Gresley 'A1', 'A10' and 'A3' class locomotives. A certain amount of renumbering took place between their first and last (BR) numbers but some of these were very short-lived. A full listing of the various numbers that have been carried by *Flying Scotsman* is included in Appendix II, but whatever it has carried, or carries in the future, it will almost certainly always be best known as No 4472.

LOCOMOTIVES BUILT AS CLASS A1

All were reboilered to become Class A3 between July 1927 and December 1948 except No 1470 which was rebuilt as Class A1/1 in September 1945. The main frames of this locomotive however were used as replacements for those on No 2573 *Harvester*.

First No	BR No	Name	Works/ Builder's No+	Year built	Date withdrawn
1470	60113	*Great Northern*	1536	1922	11/62
1471	60102	*Sir Frederick Banbury*	1539	1922	11/61
1472	60103	*Flying Scotsman*	1564	1923	1/63
1473	60104	*Solario*	1565	1923	12/59
1474	60105	*Victor Wild*	1566	1923	6/63
1475	60106	*Flying Fox*	1567	1923	12/64
1476	60107	*Royal Lancer*	1568	1923	9/63
1477	60108	*Gay Crusader*	1569	1923	10/63
1478	60109	*Hermit*	1570	1923	12/62
1479	60110	*Robert the Devil*	1571	1923	5/63
1480N	60111	*Enterprise*	1572	1923	12/62
1481N	60112	*St Simon*	1573	1923	12/64
2543	60044	*Melton*	1598	1924	6/63
2544	60045	*Lemberg*	1600	1924	11/64
2545	60046	*Diamond Jubilee*	1601	1924	6/63
2546	60047	*Donovan*	1602	1924	4/63
2547	60048	*Doncaster*	1603	1924	9/63
2548	60049	*Galtee More*	1604	1924	12/62
2549	60050	*Persimmon*	1605	1924	6/63
2550	60051	*Blink Bonny*	1606	1924	11/64
2551	60052	*Prince Palatine*	1607	1924	1/66
2552	60053	*Sansovino*	1608	1924	5/63

First No	BR No	Name	Works/ Builder's No+	Year built	Date withdrawn
2553	60054	*Prince of Wales* (*Manna* until 12/1926)	1609	1924	6/64
2554	60055	*Woolwinder*	1610	1924	9/61
2555	60056	*Centenary*	1611	1925	5/63
2556	60057	*Ormonde*	1612	1925	10/63
2557	60058	*Blair Athol*	1613	1925	6/63
2558	60059	*Tracery*	1614	1925	12/62
2559	60060	*The Tetrarch*	1615	1925	9/63
2560	60061	*Pretty Polly*	1616	1925	9/63
2561	60062	*Minoru*	1617	1925	12/64
2562	60063	*Isinglass*	1618	1925	6/64
2563	60064	*Tagalie* (*William Whitelaw* until 7/1941)	23101	1924	9/61
2564	60065	*Knight of Thistle* (*Knight of the Thistle* until 12/1932)	23102	1924	6/64
2565	60066	*Merry Hampton*	23103	1924	9/63
2566	60067	*Ladas*	23104	1924	12/62
2567	60068	*Sir Visto*	23105	1924	8/62
2568	60069	*Sceptre*	23106	1924	10/62
2569	60070	*Gladiateur*	23107	1924	5/64
2570	60071	*Tranquil*	23108	1924	10/64
2571	60072	*Sunstar*	23109	1924	10/62
2572	60073	*St Gatien*	23110	1924	8/63
2573	60074	*Harvester*	23111	1924	4/63
2574	60075	*St Frusquin*	23112	1924	1/64
2575	60076	*Galopin*	23113	1924	10/62
2576	60077	*The White Knight*	23114	1924	7/64
2577	60078	*Night Hawk*	23115	1924	10/62
2578	60079	*Bayardo*	23116	1924	9/61
2579	60080	*Dick Turpin*	23117	1924	10/64
2580	60081	*Shotover*	23118	1924	10/62
2581	60082	*Neil Gow*	23119	1924	9/63
2582	60083	*Sir Hugo*	23120	1924	5/64

LOCOMOTIVES BUILT AS CLASS A3

First No	BR No	Name	Works/ Builder's No+	Year built	Date withdrawn
2500	60035	*Windsor Lad*	1790	1934	9/61
2501	60036	*Colombo*	1791	1934	11/64
2502	60037	*Hyperion*	1792	1934	12/63
2503	60038	*Firdaussi*	1793	1934	11/63
2504	60039	*Sandwich*	1794	1934	3/63
2505	60040	*Cameronian*	1795	1934	7/64
2506	60041	*Salmon Trout*	1797	1934	12/65
2507	60042	*Singapore*	1798	1934	7/64
2508	60043	*Brown Jack*	1800	1935	5/64
2595	60084	*Trigo*	1731	1930	11/64
2596	60085	*Manna*	1733	1930	10/64
2597	60086	*Gainsborough*	1736	1930	11/63
2598	60087	*Blenheim*	1743	1930	10/63

First No	BR No	Name	Works/ Builder's No+	Year built	Date withdrawn
2599	60088	*Book Law*	1744	1930	10/63
2743	60089	*Felstead*	1693	1928	10/63
2744	60090	*Grand Parade*	1694	1928	10/63
2745	60091	*Captain Cuttle*	1695	1928	10/64
2746	60092	*Fairway*	1700	1928	10/64
2747	60093	*Coronach*	1703	1928	4/62
2748	60094	*Colorado*	1705	1928	2/64
2749	60095	*Flamingo*	1707	1929	4/61
2750	60096	*Papyrus*	1708	1929	9/63
2751	60097	*Humorist*	1709	1929	8/63
2752	60098	*Spion Kop*	1710	1929	10/63
2795	60099	*Call Boy*	1738	1930	10/63
2796	60100	*Spearmint*	1741	1930	6/65
2797	60101	*Cicero*	1742	1930	4/63

+ Nos 2563 to 2582 were built by the North British Locomotive Co Ltd, Hyde Park Works, Glasgow. All the others were built at Doncaster Works where conversions from 'A1' to 'A3' class also took place.

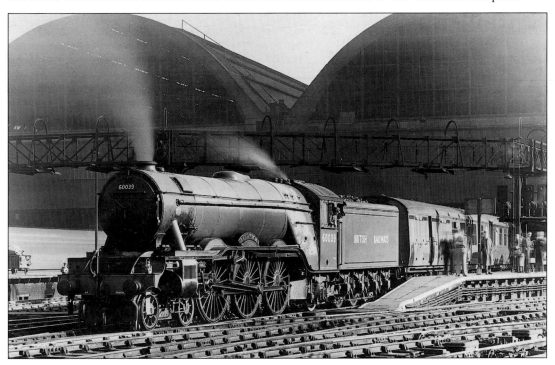

It should never be forgotten that *Flying Scotsman* was not a unique locomotive, but one of a class of 78 similar machines. It is unique today in being the sole survivor. However, other members of the class could never have achieved such worldwide fame with the names they were given. This is No 60039 *Sandwich* — which does not have quite the same 'ring' to it. *Ian Allan Library*

More often than not, *Flying Scotsman* is known as No 4472, the number it has carried, often on the side of its cab or tender side and buffer beam, for much of its life. This is in fact now one of the best known locomotive numbers anywhere in the world. Its British Railways' number, 60103, is also familiar to many but over the years several other numbers have been carried, or are applicable to this locomotive as detailed below.

Although known the world over as No 4472, and to a lesser extent, as No 60103, *Flying Scotsman's* 'pedigree' number that no owner can alter or get away from, is 1564. This is the LNER Doncaster Works number as carried on its builder's plate. *M. J. F. Bowyer*

No	Date carried	Notes
1564	1923-	LNER Doncaster Works number. Carried on an oval builder's plate affixed to the side of the smokebox but moved to the cabside when fitted with German-style smoke deflectors.
1472	24/2/23-2/3/24	Painted on cab side and front buffer beam.
4472	2/3/24-20/1/46	Painted on cab side and front buffer beam, but initially the number was carried on the side of the tender instead of the cab, where the company's coat-of-arms were displayed. This was for its two appearances at the British Empire Exhibition in 1924 and 1925. (The name *Flying Scotsman* was applied at the time of receiving the number 4472.)
502	20/1/46-5/5/46	First 1946 renumbering scheme.
103	5/5/46-15/3/48	Second 1946 renumbering scheme.
E103	15/3/48-30/12/48	First BR number. Painted on cab side and buffer beam.
60103	30/12/48-26/3/63	BR number — painted on the cab side and carried on a cast plate fitted to the smokebox door, initially above the handrail, but latterly below.
4472	26/3/63-7/93	This earlier number was reinstated when overhauled and repainted in LNER apple green livery for sale to Mr A. Pegler for preservation. Painted on buffer beam and cab side. Cabside crest applied in 10/66 with number moved to tender side. Numbers reverted to cab side in 7/73. (This number had not previously been carried since becoming Class A3.)
98872	1989-	TOPS number. Carried on inside of cab roof, for main line operational administrative purposes only.
60103	7/93-1995	BR number reinstated when restored to BR Brunswick green livery. Number painted on cab side and carried on a cast smokebox door plate, below handrail. Carried until dismantled for overhaul, late 1995.
4472	6/99-	Number reapplied following general overhaul.

In addition, on 26/11/77, this locomotive ran on the main line from York carrying the identities No 4474 *Victor Wild* and No 4480 *Enterprise*, one on each side (right and left sides respectively), during the course of the day for filming purposes in connection with the feature film *Agatha*.

Above:
Probably the most famous locomotive number in the world. Not a number of any particular distinction, it nevertheless seems to make a pleasing and easily remembered sequence of numerals.
John Titlow/Ian Allan Library

Above:
Flying Scotsman carried the number 502 for a little over three months in 1946 and as a consequence was rarely photographed as such. Also fairly short-lived was the number 103, carried from 5 May 1946 until superseded by E103 on 15 March 1948 following Nationalisation. This identity lasted only until the end of the year when it became the familiar 60103 on 30 December after BR had sorted out how it was going to number its huge, inherited fleet of locomotives. Seen as No E103 while on a running-in turn on a local train near Wakefield, 10 May 1948.
Ian Allan Library

SPECIAL SOUVENIR PLATFORM TICKET

ADMIT ONE

to view the London & North Eastern locomotive No. 4472
"Flying Scotsman" on tour with H. P. Bulmer Ltd.

Total weight 161 tons 4 cwt in working order.	Water capacity 5000 gals.
Length 70' 2¾"	Coal capacity 9 tons.
Tractive effort 32,910 lbs.	Boiler pressure 220 lbs per square inch.
Driving wheels 6' 8"	Cylinders (3) 19" x 26"

Price 10p   Nº 29205

BIBLIOGRAPHY

For such a famous locomotive surprisingly few books have been written specifically on *Flying Scotsman*. Surprising, as it can easily be assumed, because it *is* so famous, that many books must have been published. There has only been one other book, a high quality pictorial paperback, published in recent years with at least one reviewer falling into the inexcusable trap of describing it as 'yet another' *Flying Scotsman* book! An 'Ottley' is a prerequisite for a budding book reviewer. From this they will learn that the previous history of this locomotive was written by Alan Pegler et al and published by Ian Allan in its third edition in 1976.

The present book has been compiled from notes and press cuttings accumulated since Alan Pegler became an inspiration to the author by acquiring a locomotive privately for preservation. The sheer quantity of such items alone proves that this machine has had more column inches devoted to it by the media than any other machine. It has also been most interesting to see from this collection how railway publishing has developed over the past 30-odd years, from two or three staid-looking black and white magazines to today's lavish, colourful and dynamic publications. The following have all been referred to over the years and have helped to record the *Flying Scotsman* story: *Locomotives Illustrated, Modern Railways, The Railway Magazine, Railway World, Steam Railway, Steam Railway News, Trains Illustrated* and, more recently, *Heritage Railway*. Society publications include the *Railway Observer* (RCTS), *The Gresley Observer* (Gresley Society), *Swanage Railway News* and *Flying Scotsman*, the official journal of the Flying Scotsman Association. Most daily newspapers, past and present, have featured the locomotive on occasions although even in 1999 some can't really distinguish between a Gresley Pacific and a train of coaches. *Model Railway Enthusiast* magazine (No 2 December 1993) included a very detailed survey of all commercially produced models of *Flying Scotsman*.

In order to place this locomotive in its correct context, ie one of 79, and not originally unique, many books including details of Gresley Pacifics and other aspects of railway history have been referred to The following are mentioned as they contain further information on the subject in general:

A Bibliographical Dictionary of Railway Engineers, John Marshall (David & Charles, 1978)
British Pacific Locomotives, Cecil J. Allen (Ian Allan, 1962)
From Stirling to Gresley 1881-1922, F. A. S. Brown (OPC, 1974)
Gresley Locomotives A Pictorial History, Brian Haresnape (Ian Allan, 1981)
The Gresley Pacifics, Parts 1 & 2, omnibus edition, O. S. Nock (David & Charles/BCA, 1985)
Gresley Pacifics Super Profile, R. M. Tufnell (Haynes Publishing, 1985)
Locomotives of the LNER Part 2A, Tender Engines — Classes A1 to A10 (RCTS, 1978)
The Locomotives of Sir Nigel Gresley, O. S. Nock (PSL, 1991)
The Power of the A1s, A2s and A3s, J. S. Whiteley and G. W. Morrison (OPC, 1982)
Railways on the Screen, John Huntley (Ian Allan, 1993)
Speed on the East Coast Main Line, A century and a half of accelerated services, Peter Semmens (PSL, 1990)
Titled Trains of Great Britain, Cecil J. Allen (Ian Allan, 1947)
Yeadon's Register of LNER Locomotives, Vol. 1 Gresley A1 and A3 Classes, W. B. Yeadon (Irwell Press, 1990)

The following titles have been published which deal with *Flying Scotsman* exclusively:

Flying Scotsman, Alan Pegler, Cecil J. Allen, Trevor Bailey and Harold Edmonson
(Ian Allan, 1969, 1970 and 1976)
Flying Scotsman: A Locomotive Legend, Nigel Harris (Silver Link, 1988, published in Australia only)
Flying Scotsman Profile, Steve McNicol (Railmac, Australia, 1992)
Flying Scotsman on Tour Australia, John Dudley (Chapmans, 1990)
The World's Most Famous Steam Locomotive, David Clifford (Finial, 1997)

and also, for 'hours of fun':

Build Your Own Steam Locomotive (Siena, 1994) includes an 'easy-to-assemble' cardboard model of No 4472.

VIDEOGRAPHY

The preservation era has seen numerous videos released featuring this locomotive with many more sure to come. In addition to those specifically on Doncaster Works No 1564 there have been countless commercially produced videos which have included the locomotive along with other topical items. It has not been possible to view all the following so no recommendation can be given regarding quality or present availability other than for the 'official' ones now being released by Eagle Eye and which are essential viewing for all *Flying Scotsman* enthusiasts.

A Day Out with Flying Scotsman (British Nuclear Fuels, 1988)
Flying Scotsman: A Journey to the Red Heart of Australia (Videolines, 1991)
Flying Scotsman on Preserved Lines 1994/95 (Lumic Video Productions, 1995)
Flying Scotsman: The Most Famous Steam Locomotive (Australian tour) (Simitar, 1991)
On Tour Australia 1988 (Eagle Eye)
Preserving the Legend (Bygone Films, 1994 — reissued by Eagle Eye)
The Restoration of Flying Scotsman Parts 1-6 (Eagle Eye, 1997-9)
Tender Memories (Bygone Films, 1996 — reissued by Eagle Eye)

USEFUL ADDRESSES

Internet: http://www.flyingscotsman.com

Flying Scotsman Railways Limited,
PO Box 4472, Lichfield, Staffordshire WS13 6GR
Tel 01543 250865
Fax 01543 417531
For train information and bookings.

Flying Scotsman Railways Ltd,
Southall Depot, Glade Lane, Southall, Middx UB2 4PL
Tel 02085 744472 (Contact: Roland Kennington)
For volunteers wishing to participate in the work at Southall. (No casual visitors.)

Flying Scotsman Association,
PO Box 4472, East Oxford DO, OX4 4WT
Tel 01865 784600 (Contact: Clare Dewell, Secretary)
e-mail cdewell@oxmol.co.uk
For membership enquiries.

Eagle Eye Productions,
51 Railway Side, Barnes, London SW13 0PN
Flying Scotsman videos.

The Gresley Society
The Secretary, Peter Rodgers,
Manor Cottage, Birkby,
Northallerton DL7 0EF
The society exists to promote
interest in the work of
Sir Nigel Gresley.

The Gresley Trust,
Sycamore House, Station Lane, Shipton-by-Beningbrough, York YO6 1AG
Formed to attract support and funds to ensure the continued existence of surviving locomotives and rolling stock designed by Sir Nigel Gresley.

Considering the fame and travels of *Flying Scotsman*, and the number of 'personal appearances' made, surprisingly few items have been produced in the past bearing the locomotive's image. This situation is being rectified by the new owner, with many quality items depicting the locomotive now available. *Author*

No 4472 at Epstone, 12 January 1986. *Colour-Rail*